Popular Science
DECKS & SUN SPACES

Alfred Lees with Ernest V. Heyn

Popular Science
DECKS & SUN SPACES

Alfred Lees with Ernest V. Heyn

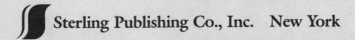 Sterling Publishing Co., Inc.   New York

Library of Congress Cataloging-in-Publication Data

Lees, Alfred W.
  Popular science decks & sunspaces.

  Includes index.
  1. Decks (Architecture, Domestic)—Design and
construction.   2. Sunspaces—Design and construction.
I. Heyn, Ernest Victor, 1904–   .   II. Title.
III. Title: Popular science decks and sunspaces.
TH4970.L44   1991   690'.89   90-10380
ISBN 0-8069-7448-6

Designed by Jeff Fitschen

10   9   8   7   6   5   4   3   2   1

Published in 1991 by Sterling Publishing Company, Inc.
387 Park Avenue South, New York, N.Y. 10016

Introductions, new text and photographs
© 1991 by Alfred Lees
Distributed in Canada by Sterling Publishing
℅ Canadian Manda Group, P.O. Box 920, Station U
Toronto, Ontario, Canada M8Z 5P9
Distributed in Great Britain and Europe by Cassell PLC
Villiers House, 41/47 Strand, London WC2N 5JE, England
Distributed in Australia by Capricorn Ltd.
P.O. Box 665, Lane Cove, NSW 2066
Printed and bound in Hong Kong
All rights reserved

ISBN 0-8069-7448-6

Contents

II Sunspaces, Sun Porches, Sun Rooms   147

Popular Science DECKS & SUN SPACES

Alfred Lees with Ernest V. Heyn

Introduction

Within the last decade, decks became the number one home improvement across America. As the costs for new housing spiraled up beyond the reach of many home buyers, increasing the size of one's current house became a top priority. What had long been standard practice—trading up to a larger house as the family grew—was no longer an option in many cases. Budgets dictated that families stay put and expand the home they already owned. The most accessible means of doing this was by adding a deck. For most homes, such a project can be undertaken with minimal disruption to daily living, and at moderate cost. Best of all, this is a project most homeowners can tackle themselves.

Unlike a room addition, a deck involves no elaborate foundation, no smashing through an existing wall, no fussy joints where a new roof intersects the old. Yet the space gained with such an "outdoor room" can be utilized for much of the year—except in severe climate zones.

In these areas, the same factors led to another development in U.S. home improvement—the glass-enclosed sunspace. The initial boost for this type of add-on came with popular interest in lessening the shock of rising fuel costs by taking advantage of passive solar energy. The home greenhouse was promoted as a contribution to home heating—assuming it could be sited on the sunny south side of the house and had a built-in solar mass: a ceramic-tiled concrete floor or masonry wall that would absorb daylight heat to radiate into the space after sundown. Even though there is now less interest in this aspect, the sunspace retains its popularity. People who've been guests in homes with a sunspace often come away determined to add one to their own home.

For this reason, sunspaces are coming to be recognized as a housing plus—an addition that can increase a home's resale value. There's been no question for some years now that *decks* add value to homes. Decks are a feature that attracts prospective home buyers. And if a sunspace has been properly designed and installed, it can similarly enhance the value of a home.

Though this book is a collection of specific projects, it also dispenses general information about both types of add-ons. No outdoor construction should ever be built of lumber that's not resistant to rot, and this truism applies emphatically to a structure as exposed to weathering as an open deck. If you're not building it of naturally-resistant redwood or cedar, your lumber should be pressure-treated. Your fasteners and connectors should all resist rust; if they're not costly stainless steel or aluminum, they should be hot-dipped galvanized. Whichever lumber you choose, the deck, bench and railing planks should be laid bark-side up, to avoid cupping, which would retain water. (Just check the end grain of each plank, and place it so that the growth rings curve down.)

When it comes to sunspaces, only durable materials with long-lasting seals should be used, and careful planning to avoid the excess heat and humidity we've all associated with greenhouses at nurseries and botanical gardens is a must. The major difference between an old-style greenhouse and a modern sunspace is that while the former was intended for "hot-house" plants, the latter is designed for human comfort.

This book not only presents the widest possible variety of deck and sunspace *designs*—with detailed dimensioned drawings when the project is applicable to many homes—it also addresses the maintenance and accessorizing of such add-ons. For good measure, it includes detached garden structures, plus glassed-in areas that don't technically function as sunspaces: sun rooms, solariums, sun porches.

How was such a book born? While Ernest V. Heyn was Editor-in-Chief of *Popular Science*—a monthly magazine founded in 1872—he proposed a plan to recycle in book form the do-it-yourself projects and instructions from that magazine. Since his retirement, he's led a busy life working on this franchise, which came to be known as the "Heyn Line of PS Books." The volume you hold in your hands in the tenth—and last—in this series. In many respects, it marks the end of an era.

When Mr. Heyn first asked me to propose a subject for a new volume in his series, I was still the editor in charge of all do-it-yourself material for *Popular Science*, and I quickly told him that I'd devoted the best of my DIY pages in recent years to a variety of decks. "They're the quintessential home-improvement project, Ernie," I explained, "and PS readers keep asking for more." During the late 80's (I announced early retirement—after 35 years as a how-to editor—at the end of 1988) I had scheduled at least one deck project in every issue from spring to fall and had accumulated the best selection ever published. In the June '88 issue I had climaxed this collection by publishing the results of a national design contest I'd set up to smoke out the best "problem-solving" decks in America (I've chosen to open Part I of this book with those prizewinning designs).

While Mr. Heyn was properly impressed with my devotion to decks (he knew I'd built several myself) he put off proposing his new book to a publisher until it could be rounded out with a complementary category of projects. And he knew he'd found that when he saw the special section on sunspaces I'd devised, with the help of my PS colleagues, for the September '88 issue. He burst into my office clutching an advance copy of that issue and shouted: "Decks and sunspaces! We have our book!" I then set out to select the best of the PS projects in both categories and my retirement has made it possible for me to edit, update and—where necessary—rewrite these articles for this book.

The executives of *Popular Science*, meanwhile, have paid me the ultimate compliment of not replacing me at the magazine. They've decided, instead, to limit the editorial focus to science, technology and automotive subjects, and thus no longer publish the type of article I spent 25 years developing for them. So there will be no further material for project or how-to books, and I'm only happy that this last volume in the Heyn Line has turned out to be the best in the series.

As noted on the title page, most of the dimensioned drawings for the projects in this book were commissioned from America's top technical draftsman, Carl De Groote, and this book would not have been possible without my years of collaboration with this artist. Unfailingly, Carl has taken my scruffy sketches and building site scribbles and transformed them into clear, logical plans that are a joy to study and build from. Carl has raised technical draftsmanship to the level of fine art, and I was disheartened to learn, as this book went to press, that the project magazines for whom Carl free-lances are urging him to "computerize, like everyone else." The personal distinctiveness that Carl (and the handful of other fine draftsmen whose work appears herein)* always brought to project pages during my 35 years in publishing is about to be homogenized into a charac-

---

*These other artists are individually identified at the end of any text that Carl *didn't* illustrate; drawings that accompany texts without an art credit are all the work of DeGroote.

terless general competence. So in yet another respect, this book marks the end of an era.

A final word of appreciation to the various lumber associations and national wood-product companies whose cooperation over the many years made projects on the scale of those in this book possible. Without the editorial-promotion budgets of the California Redwood Assn., American Plywood Assn., and Georgia-Pacific, the more spectacular decks and structures featured here would have remained beyond my practical reach. Of course it's been the intent of these organizations to inspire more homeowners to buy their lumber products, just as it was mine to sell more magazines (and now books) by making my projects as irresistible as possible. Let's hope we've all succeeded.

Sprinkled through these texts are addresses of sources that can supply special materials the projects call for, or additional help. Finally, these texts are signed either by the freelancers who submitted the original articles or by PS staff writers (past and present) who helped me prepare them for publication in the magazine. The latter include Dave Houser, Dawn Stover, Naomi Freundlich, Tim Bakke and Elaine Gilmore. It's been a pleasure working with such talented people, as well as with my editors at Sterling Publishing. Thanks, too, to Ernie Heyn for persisting in his search for the right publisher; and to Ron Nelson, without whom this book could not have been compiled.

We've collaborated on a fine book, here, gang; may it heighten backyard pleasures across the country! And was e'er an era's end more fittingly marked?

Alfred Lees
President, National Assn. of Home and Workshop Writers and retired Home and Shop Editor of Popular Science

I Decks and Yard Shelters

Today's major family living problem is likely to be lack of space. In the contemporary "affordable" home, the dining room and the den have disappeared—and where do you entertain batches of guests without that long-gone "family room"? The quickest and least costly way to expand is to add an *outdoor* room: either an attached deck, open to the sky, or a freestanding roofed structure such as a gazebo. With modern materials and products, deck building and maintenance is easier than ever. Here are over 30 designs for attached decks—low patio-style or lofty elevated decks—that, while adding gracious space, tackle many other problems as well, soaring over steep sites . . . wrapping around trees, pools and spas . . . hiding ugly concrete slabs. And if an attached deck isn't right for your site, here are ideas for yard shelters, too.

1 Five Prizewinning Deck Designs

Are the deck designs on these pages the shrewdest in America? When the California Redwood Association and I set up the parameters for this national design competition we deliberately kept the qualifications as broad as it was practical to make them. For those homeowners who'd be building a deck especially for the contest, we didn't want to inhibit creativity. And where professional contractors were concerned, we wished to avoid making them fear that their more innovative projects were too far-out to qualify. So except for requiring that redwood be the dominant material, we asked only that the deck solve at least one difficult problem: taming an unbuildable site, providing built-in storage, concealing an eyesore, or whatever. The contest was announced in *Popular Science* with the deadline for entries five months later.

The response was spectacular (see page 23), and these are the five winners I chose with judges from the California Redwood Assn. We were able to inspect the top winners in person while rephotographing them and were delighted with the workmanship. Of the top three prizewinners, the first two decks were designed and built by professionals, the third was designed and built entirely by the homeowners.

- The grand prizewinner is the work of a creative young designer/contractor, Bryan Brylka, for a house that perches at the crest of a steep forested hillside. It's a strikingly original solution to the problem of combining deck spaces with a ramped access to an elaborate hot tub far below. The "spokes" that radiate from the tub across the surrounding redwood deck are ¼-inch Plexiglas acrylic plastic strips laminated between the planks. Though they are sanded flush with the deck surface (which is then

Ramps, platforms, and rails are finished with Cuprinol Heavy Duty Deck Stain in chestnut brown. Bottom section of lower ramp hinges up to reveal a bar.

GRAND PRIZEWINNER

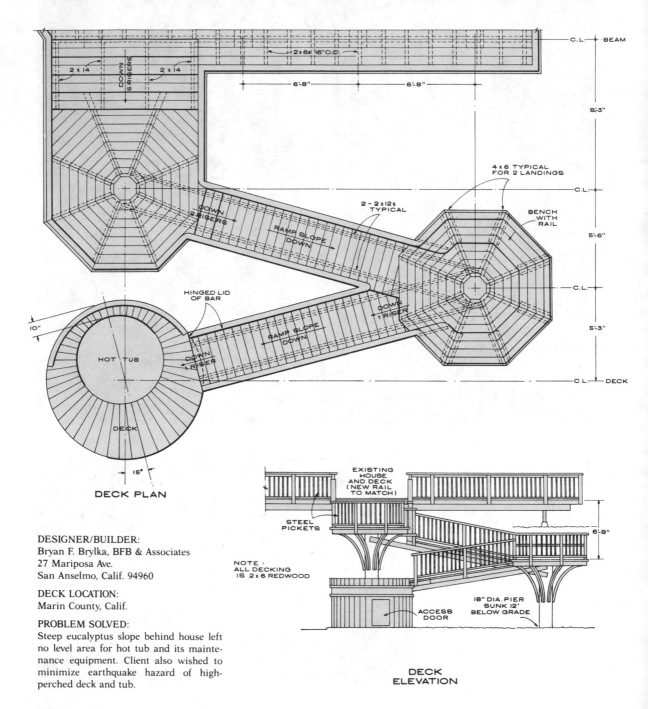

2 x 6s 16" O.C.

C.L. — BEAM

2 x 14   DOWN 6 RISERS   2 x 14

6'-8"   6'-8"

8'-3"

4 x 6 TYPICAL
FOR 2 LANDINGS

C.L.

DOWN 2 RISERS

2 - 2 x 12s
TYPICAL

BENCH
WITH
RAIL

RAMP SLOPE
DOWN

5'-6"

HINGED LID
OF BAR

C.L.

DOWN 1 RISER

10"

DOWN 1 RISER

RAMP SLOPE
DOWN

5'-3"

HOT TUB

DECK

C.L. — DECK

15°

DECK PLAN

DESIGNER/BUILDER:
Bryan F. Brylka, BFB & Associates
27 Mariposa Ave.
San Anselmo, Calif. 94960

DECK LOCATION:
Marin County, Calif.

PROBLEM SOLVED:
Steep eucalyptus slope behind house left
no level area for hot tub and its maintenance equipment. Client also wished to
minimize earthquake hazard of high-
perched deck and tub.

EXISTING
HOUSE
AND DECK
(NEW RAIL
TO MATCH)

STEEL
PICKETS

NOTE:
ALL DECKING
IS 2 x 6 REDWOOD

6'-9"

ACCESS
DOOR

18" DIA. PIER
SUNK 12'
BELOW GRADE

DECK
ELEVATION

16

SECOND PRIZEWINNER A

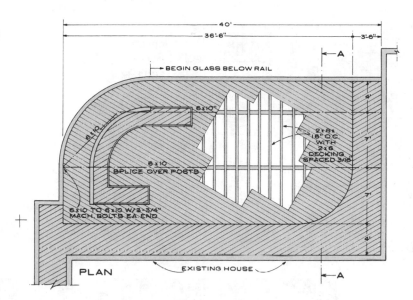

PLAN

- 40'
- 36'-6"
- 3'-6"
- BEGIN GLASS BELOW RAIL
- 6 x 10
- 6 x 10
- 6 x 10 SPLICE OVER POSTS
- 2 x R's 18" O.C. WITH 2 x 6 DECKING SPACED 3/8"
- 6 x 10 TO 6 x 10 W/ 3-3/4" MACH. BOLTS EA. END
- A
- A
- EXISTING HOUSE
- 4'
- 7'
- 7'
- 4'

Substructure was engineered by Bob Martin.

DESIGNER/BUILDER:
Gary Marsh
All Decked Out
770 Tamalpais Ave.
Novato, Calif. 94947

DECK LOCATION:
Larkspur, Calif.

PROBLEM SOLVED:
Existing non-redwood deck was falling from house and undermined by mud slides; solid railing obscured mountain view for those seated inside. New deck was stepped down from living room with tempered glass railing and was cantilevered over the slide area.

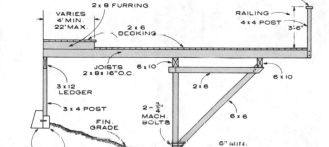

SECTION "A-A"

- 2 x 8 CAP
- RAILING 4 x 4 POST
- 3'-6"
- 2 x 8 FURRING
- VARIES 4' MIN. 22' MAX.
- 2 x 6 DECKING
- JOISTS 2 x 8s 16" O.C.
- 6 x 10
- 6 x 10
- 2 x 6
- 6 x 6
- 3 x 12 LEDGER
- 3 x 4 POST
- 2 – 3/4" MACH. BOLTS
- FIN. GRADE
- 6" MIN.
- EXIST. HOUSE FOOTING
- NEW POST FOOTING 6" x 18" ATTACH TO EXIST. FOOTING WITH "J" BOLTS
- FIN. GRADE
- B

SECT. "B"

- N° 3 TIES AT 18"
- 18"
- VERT. 4 - N° 5 RE-BAR
- 9"
- CONCRETE
- 12'
- B
- 18"

SOIL BEARING TESTING DETERMINES DEPTH OF PIER

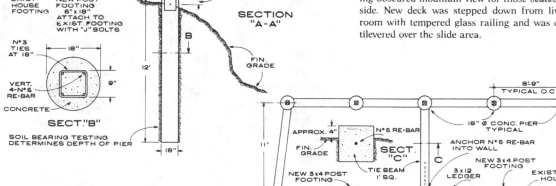

FOUNDATION PLAN

- 8'-9" TYPICAL O.C.
- 3'
- 11'
- APPROX. 4"
- FIN. GRADE
- N° 5 RE-BAR
- **SECT. "C"**
- TIE BEAM 1' SQ.
- NEW 3 x 4 POST FOOTING
- 3 x 12 LEDGER
- 18" Ø CONC. PIER TYPICAL
- ANCHOR N° 5 RE-BAR INTO WALL
- NEW 3 x 4 POST FOOTING
- EXISTING HOUSE
- C
- C

SECOND PRIZEWINNER B

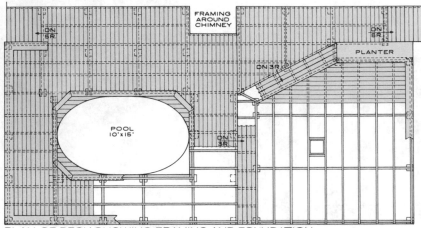

PLAN OF DECK SHOWING FRAMING AND FOUNDATION

POOL 10'x15'

DESIGNER:
Jain Moon

BUILDER:
Scott Foell

DECK LOCATION:
Novato, Calif.

PROBLEM SOLVED:
Poor soil prevented excavating for a swimming pool, so the entire yard was decked around an above-ground pool. Filter is housed at hinged corner, and other service access is through side hatches. Privacy from neighbors is provided by planters and trellis.

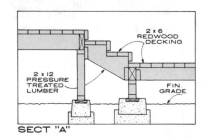

SECT "A"

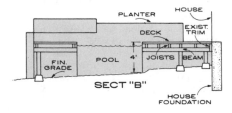

SECT "B"

Raised portion gives the look of an in-ground pool. Hinged corner gives access to filter (below).

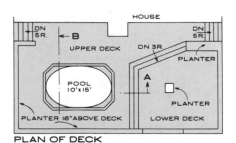

PLAN OF DECK

18

The grand prizewinner has octagonal pods supported on concrete piers by means of boomerang braces laminated from strips of redwood and fir.

On second prizewinner A (above), glass-paneled railing doesn't hide the view. Curved top rails are pieced. Second prizewinner B (right) is stained gray to match the house siding, this deck covers the entire backyard.

THIRD PRIZEWINNER A

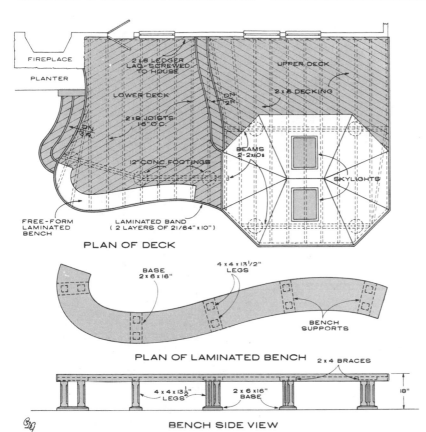

FIREPLACE

PLANTER

2 x 8 LEDGER LAG-SCREWED TO HOUSE

UPPER DECK

LOWER DECK

DN 2R

2 x 6 DECKING

2 x 8 JOISTS 16" O.C.

DN 3R

12" CONC. FOOTINGS

BEAMS 2-2 x 10s

SKYLIGHTS

FREE-FORM LAMINATED BENCH

LAMINATED BAND (2 LAYERS OF 21/64" x 10")

PLAN OF DECK

BASE 2 x 6 x 16"

4 x 4 x 13½" LEGS

BENCH SUPPORTS

PLAN OF LAMINATED BENCH

2 x 4 BRACES

4 x 4 x 13½" LEGS

2 x 6 x 16" BASE

18"

BENCH SIDE VIEW

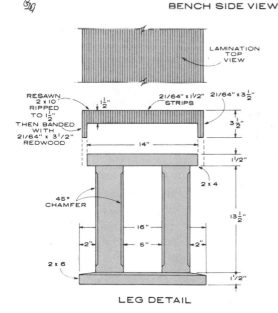

LAMINATION TOP VIEW

RESAWN 2 x 10 RIPPED TO 1½" THEN BANDED WITH 21/64" x 3½" REDWOOD

1½"

21/64" x 1½" 21/64" x 3½" STRIPS

3½"

14"

1½"

2 x 4

45° CHAMFER

16"

13½"

2" 5" 2"

2 x 6

1½"

LEG DETAIL

DESIGNER/BUILDER:
Ben Sechrist
Box 361
Manchester, Maine 04351

DECK LOCATION:
Manchester, Maine.

PROBLEM SOLVED:
Homeowner wanted to level off a sloping lakeside site for a sheltered spa—in a way that would halt minor erosion beside house. Builder notched pressure-treated joists at high end of deck into soil as retainers, erected skylighted gazebo around the spa, then created free-form deck—railed with laminated redwood bench—to match informality of the house.

Free-form lakeside deck in Maine has bench laminated from redwood strips.

THIRD PRIZEWINNER B

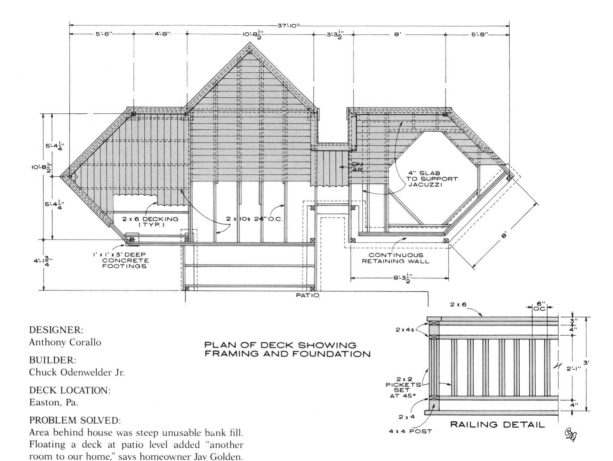

PLAN OF DECK SHOWING FRAMING AND FOUNDATION

- 37'-10"
- 5'-6"
- 4'-8"
- 10'-8½"
- 3'-3½"
- 8'
- 5'-8"
- 5'-4¼"
- 10'-8½"
- 5'-4¼"
- 4'-1¾"
- 2 x 6 DECKING (TYP.)
- 2 x 10s 24" O.C.
- 1' x 1' x 3' DEEP CONCRETE FOOTINGS
- DN 4R
- 4" SLAB TO SUPPORT JACUZZI
- CONTINUOUS RETAINING WALL
- 8'-3½"
- 8'
- PATIO

RAILING DETAIL

- 2 x 6
- 6" O.C.
- 2 x 4s
- 3¾"
- 2 x 2 PICKETS SET AT 45°
- 2'-1"
- 3'
- 2 x 4
- 4"
- 4 x 4 POST

DESIGNER:
Anthony Corallo

BUILDER:
Chuck Odenwelder Jr.

DECK LOCATION:
Easton, Pa.

PROBLEM SOLVED:
Area behind house was steep unusable bank fill. Floating a deck at patio level added "another room to our home," says homeowner Jay Golden. The railing around the raised spa deck provides an anchor for a gate to keep out unattended children.

Triple-prow deck floats off a Pennsylvania hill. Section at right has spa sunk into it. Unique railing ties it all together.

sealed with multiple coats of clear epoxy), the strips project an inch below the deck's underside, where a light source illuminates them as well as the water in the tub.

- For his project, Gary Marsh of All Decked Out inherited an existing deteriorating deck with underpinnings weakened by a landslide. For the replacement deck, a bracing system had to be developed to support a center-point beam over which the deck could cantilever. Even with these piers set well back from the edge of the cliff, the engineer drilled 32-feet-deep to reach stable soil, then tied the piers and the house foundation together.

- When Jain Moon designed a platform deck around her above-ground pool, this raised the "backyard" 4 feet and compromised the privacy provided by existing fences. So Moon and builder Scott Foell cleverly included trellised planters at the perimeter of the decking. For the trellis top, 4-foot 2 × 4s were cut in half at a 30-degree angle to slant down on both sides of the double beam.

- Maine builder Ben Sechrist's client wanted an underused yard leveled so that a shed sunspace with a hot tub inside could be added to the house. Ben proposed instead an open deck with a gazebo at one end to shelter the hot tub. This took the form of a stretched octagon. Skylights on both long sides of the steep roof flank a vented cupola. All openings are screened against lakeside insects.

- The Golden project in Pennyslvania used (like the other four) redwood decking and railings supported on framing of pressure-treated lumber. Deck boards were fastened with hot-dipped galvanized nails; all bolts were stainless steel.—*Text by Alfred Lees.*

Winnowing down several hundred entries to the 25 from which the final selections were made wasn't easy. In this task, author Alfred Lees (at right) and CRA's publicity manager, Charlene Draheim (center), were joined by Christopher Grover, CRA's promotion manager. The entries they're evaluating came from 32 states, with greatest representation from California (not unexpectedly), followed by Colorado and Montana. The prairie states also scored high, with the lightest participation from the East Coast (though two winners came from there). Lees and CRA devoted three days to the final judging and reported that those last hours of decision-making—narrowing the field to five—were excruciating.

2 Three Decks for Impossible Sites

What good is a backyard you can't enjoy? Whether a yard is steeply sloped, overgrown with vegetation, or just too ugly to be inviting, it's useless space. It increases your property tax without contributing anything to your lifestyle.

But summon Cary Recker, a muscular deck-building specialist from Atlanta, Ga., and your useless backyard can be transformed into the focal point of your house. Recker designs and constructs "impossible" decks on what might be considered hopeless sites.

Take deck A, for example. Here, Recker confronted a backyard 26 feet below the house's main living area. To make matters worse, the site was buried in primitive forest. A carpenter with guts was needed—one who was both acrobat and jungle fighter.

In the case of deck B, the backyard was a steep slope terraced with more than 500 railroad ties for $20,000 worth of landscaping. Obviously, the deck job called for more than superior building skills. Fine decorative taste was required, too.

For deck C, a concrete patio had outlived its usefulness. A once-small family had grown, with in-laws and grandchildren visiting each summer. Space was needed for outdoor entertaining, but the slab was edged with low brick walls that prevented any extension. This job called for a demolition expert.

Though widely varied, the assignments all drew on Recker's basic belief that a deck should make an architectural statement. "Most people who build decks just jut a square or rectangle from the back of the house," he says. "I've yet to build a square deck. All my decks are custom-shaped to their site. And the design may be adapted as I build."

Deck A was originally intended to extend 8 feet from one

"I wanted deck A (right) to float above the jungle as if hung from a helicopter," says Recker of the deck at right. Decks B and C cover special problems: one stands on a steep site (bottom left) and the other over a grim patio slab (bottom right).

DECK A

DECK B

DECK C

DECK A

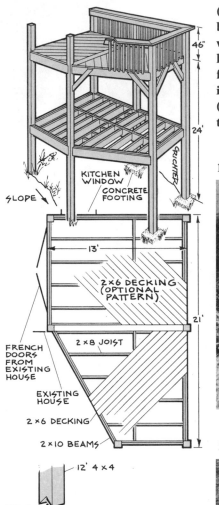

46"

24'

SLOPE

KITCHEN WINDOW

CONCRETE FOOTING

SLICHTER

13'

2×6 DECKING (OPTIONAL PATTERN)

21'

FRENCH DOORS FROM EXISTING HOUSE

2×8 JOIST

EXISTING HOUSE

2×6 DECKING

2×10 BEAMS

12' 4×4

NOTCH

2×4

2×6

45°

14' 4×4

POST DETAIL

2×6 ON FLAT

2×6 ON EDGE

2×6 DECK

46"

2×2s 6" O.C.

RAILING DETAIL

(1) Plywood boxes are forms for concrete footings, located by laying out shape of deck with twine. (2) Bulked-up wooden posts are set into concrete piers. (3) In corner of house, ledgers meet atop a post lag-bolted to the concrete foundation. (4) Joist pattern is similar on both levels; ¾-inch ply is loose-laid on lower level as a work platform. (5) Skewed right side adds design interest. (6) Knee braces to posts firm up the 26-foot-high upper deck.

1

2

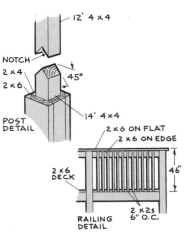

3

4   5   6

Editor's note: Each builder develops an individual approach to construction—and some prejudices. Recker's reservations concerning joist hangers are not confirmed by the experience of PS editors. But Koppers Corp. (major franchiser of pressure treatments) recommends using a water repellent on Wolmanized lumber after 6 months, as Recker does.

corner of the house at a 45-degree angle. As Recker dug his footings, however, he uncovered an underground stream. To bridge it, he extended the deck another 4 feet at a 60-degree angle.

Deck B stands a foot high where it takes off from a ledger attached to the house. But by the time it extends 26 feet, it's over 12 feet off the ground.

"It was designed like an observation deck on the side of a mountain," Recker says. "With the yard's dramatic slope, the bow shape—like the front of a ship—gives an ideal vantage point for viewing the yard."

To add visual interest to deck C, built over a nondescript patio tucked into an L-shaped ranch, Recker built it on two levels, notching out one corner for a large tree. "The idea here was to create a natural addition to the house," he says. "That's why most of the deck lacks a railing, and the benches are low enough to sit on facing either in or out."

Recker also has strong opinions when it comes to construction techniques. "Even though a deck is your eyeball on the world," he says, "it should be built for safety first and the best view second." For Recker, safety means taking no chances on structural integrity. "When in doubt, overbuild," he says, "especially when your deck is more than a couple of feet high."

Some of Recker's construction methods are "above and beyond the call of duty." For instance, he obtains maximum anchorage for posts by setting them directly into wet concrete.

Recker favors plywood boxes for footing forms, and he sets them at least a foot deep—below local frost lines. The posts for deck A were set directly on bedrock, a granite vein 5 feet down. To keep posts elevated and level as the concrete in the forms sets, Recker tacks a 2 × 4 brace to each side of the post, with stakes driven into the ground to anchor the opposite ends.

27

DECK B

Under-deck-storage swing-in lattice panel is framed and hinged to the central stile. Bow bench is formed by nailing angled 2 × 4s to the rail posts, then adding horizontal cross members and nailing on 2 × 6 planks.

2 × 6 RAIL

EXISTING HOUSE

4'6"

8'

8'

8'

45°

BENCH 3 2 × 6S WIDE

26'

4'

4'

4'

10'

8'

HINGED PANEL FOR UNDER-DECK STORAGE

BENCH DETAIL

18"

VERT. POST

2 × 4 FRAME

35°

4'

2 × 10

(1) Support structure was tied together with lattice; large under-deck area can be used for storage. Two panels can be hinged for access. (2) Lower panels were cut to follow ground contour; steps were provided next to the house. (3) Outer half-hex railing doubles as a backrest for a built-in bench of 2 × 6s nailed over a support frame of 2 × 4s.

DECK C

Diagonal joist is an assembly that, when capped with a 2 × 6, leaves a ledger on each side to which the angle-cut deck planks can be nailed.

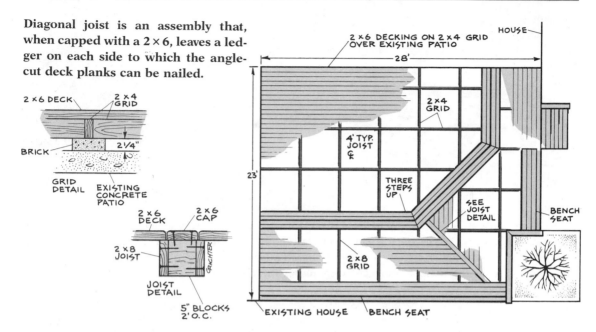

2 × 6 DECK   2 × 4 GRID

BRICK   2¼"

GRID DETAIL   EXISTING CONCRETE PATIO

2 × 6 DECK   2 × 6 CAP

2 × 8 JOIST

JOIST DETAIL

5" BLOCKS 2' O.C.

2 × 6 DECKING ON 2 × 4 GRID OVER EXISTING PATIO   HOUSE

28'

2 × 4 GRID

4' TYP. JOIST ℄

23'

THREE STEPS UP

SEE JOIST DETAIL

BENCH SEAT

2 × 8 GRID

EXISTING HOUSE   BENCH SEAT

Recker shuns the notion of setting posts after the deck is built. "Temporary posts tend to warp the deck," he claims, "and posts can sink further into the ground, causing a deck to separate from the house." His footings will set at least a week before Recker knocks the braces down.

For even greater safety on a tall deck, Recker may also attach posts to the wall of the existing house, as shown in the photos for deck A. For beams and ledgers, Recker prefers 2 × 8s, 2 × 10s, or even 2 × 12s—and he doubles the thickness when the deck height is more than 4 feet. When possible, he face-nails beams into posts with 20-penny nails; to secure ledgers he drives 3½-inch anchor bolts into lead anchors spaced 1½ feet apart. For deck A, he wrapped the 4 × 4 posts with 2 × 6s and 2 × 4s on opposing sides, face-nailed right up beneath the beams.

Even more unorthodox is Recker's refusal to use joist hangers without reinforcing them. "Joist hangers are good for keeping joists flush with the top of beams," he says. "Structurally, you should come in with face nails. A strip of wood—at least a 2 × 2 running under the joists as a ledger—is still more insurance."

29

(1) Recker floats a 4-by-4-foot grid over the slab, resting on concrete bricks under the joints. (2) Brawn takes care of restricting walls so the deck can extend past the existing slab. (3) Raised deck section is framed out from a diagonal beam supported (where Recker stands) on a post and pier. (4) Framing scheme permits lively pattern in deck planks; note angled steps between two levels.

For best drainage, Recker nails his deck planks so the grain rings at the ends cup down. He also checks both ends of a board to be sure that the grain cups the same way. If it doesn't, the board was cut diagonally from the log, which may lead to warping.

Even though he always uses pressure-treated lumber, Recker recommends that decks receive some sort of treatment after six months. "After all," he says, "I expect them to last longer than the houses they're attached to."—*Text by Doug Traub; photos by the author and Ann Recker; drawings by Gerhard Richter.*

3 Get the Most from a Small Deck

Getting the most from a small deck can mean building one from scratch to serve a special need, or redesigning an existing one to increase its contribution to your outdoor living. The three approaches on the following pages have one thing in common: You can complete the work in a week or two.

HIGH-RISE DECK FOR A LOW-RISE HOUSE

Sure, a patio or ground-floor deck is often the fastest, least-expensive way to add space for entertaining. But the backyard of my ranch house was easily visible from adjacent yards—and it isn't a good-neighbor policy to erect high screens.

Roof's extended overhang required 18-inch threaded steel rods to connect deck beams to wall plate (above).

HIGH-RISE DECK FOR A LOW-RISE HOUSE

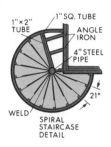

1" × 2" TUBE
1" SQ. TUBE
ANGLE IRON
4" STEEL PIPE
WELD
21°
SPIRAL STAIRCASE DETAIL

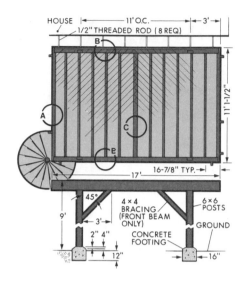

HOUSE
11' O.C.
3'
1/2" THREADED ROD (8 REQ)
B
11' 1-1/2"
A
C
B
16-7/8" TYP.
17'
45°
9'
3'
2" 4"
12"
4 × 4 BRACING (FRONT BEAM ONLY)
CONCRETE FOOTING
6 × 6 POSTS
GROUND
16"

2 × 4
2 × 12
DETAIL **A**

2 × 12
2 × 10
DETAIL **B**

2 × 4
2 × 8
DETAIL **C**

The solution: the ultimate deck—a second-story deck for a single-story house. An elevated deck would give me privacy and an unobstructed view of a sight I never tire of: the bright lights of nearby Las Vegas. But you don't need a low-slung house to get the most from an elevated deck—all you need is a vista to enjoy and a little imagination.

I decided to keep my raised redwood deck small, in scale with the house. But several features—a spiral staircase, two types of railings, and decking applied diagonally—add distinction. I began construction by securing four 6 × 6 posts to concrete footings. I used two types of beams: at front and rear, a 2 × 12 backed up by two 2 × 10s; for the sides, a single 2 × 12. I used eight ½-inch threaded rods to anchor the deck through the top plate of my house. If you can lag-screw a ledger directly to existing framing, construction is even easier. Angle braces on the outer 6 × 6 posts give additional lateral support.

To enjoy the city view while sitting, I installed see-through front railings. Instead of wood, I decided to try something different: metal. I drilled holes in the horizontal 2 × 4s to accept ⅝-inch-steel rods, primed and painted to match the redwood lumber. For the side and back rails, 1 × 6s were sufficient for maintaining privacy and blocking wind.

The top of the stair pole is attached to the deck with lag bolts through welded-on angle iron; the bottom is set in concrete. To create the curved metal handrail for the stairs, I used ⅛-by-¾-inch strap steel, which is flexible. I bent three straps side by side in place and welded them together and to the 1-inch-square tubing uprights to form a railing. If you're not a welder, install a commercial stair.

UNDER DECK SCREEN HOUSE

An elevated deck is a great place to laze away summer hours—except when it rains. So I decided to put my small, second-story deck to fuller use by building a screen house underneath. Construction costs? $350.

I began by sinking pressure-treated horizontal 4 × 4 sills slightly into the ground and toenailing them to the existing deck posts. Then I framed in the screen doors and installed studs between the posts (spacing depends on available screen widths, although it shouldn't exceed 40 inches). I toenailed horizontal screen supports to the vertical supports 38 inches above the ground. Horizontal supports align with the bars on the screen door.

Screen house makes use of deck in rain or shine. Floor is 1½-inch layer of crushed stone, easy to maintain.

33

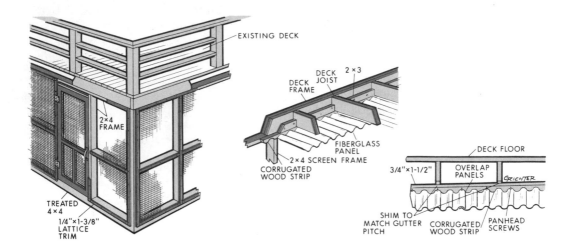

To handle rainwater draining through the slats of the deck, I built a ceiling of corrugated fiberglass panels that guides rainwater into a gutter nailed to the house studs. I sloped the gutter ¼-inch per foot along the house wall, then installed the corrugated fiberglass panels, pitched ¼-to ½-inch per foot toward the house, or about three inches for my 10-foot span. (The panels were also pitched to one side to match the slope of the gutter.) For ceiling support—and to ensure efficient drainage—I overlapped the fiberglass panels onto the gutter by 1½ inches.

To secure the other end of the panels, I used shaped wood strips (sold for use with corrugated panels) fastened to 2×3s nailed to the joists. The panels were also supported in the center of the ceiling, midway between the front and rear walls (see drawing). I used shims where necessary to maintain the proper pitch toward the gutter.

I fastened the fiberglass panels—making sure to overlap the joints by a curved segment, or wave—to the wood strips with panhead screws. As decoration, I hung several 2×4 "suspended" beams that run the length of the screen house.

I stapled the screens to the frame at 6-inch intervals and then trimmed with ¼-by-1⅜-inch lattice to cover staples and sharp edges. Finally, I hooked up the gutter to my roof's drain system and installed a screen door at each end of the screen house.

DECK EXTENSION

The only thing one could say about the original deck was that it came with the house. Its plain, unimaginative design did nothing to encourage use. The small, 10-by-10-foot space seemed crowded with a couple of chairs, so entertaining there was impossible. And the deck wasn't well-planned: The stairs, for example, led *away* from the slab patio below.

I thought of tearing down the deck and starting from scratch, but that approach—while it would have relieved my frustrations—would have robbed me of a back entry for weeks and cost too much. The less-expensive solution? Keep the structure intact, but extend the deck, adding design features and rerouted stairs. In a week, the original deck was 10-feet wider and completely renovated.

Construction began with footings for new 4×4 posts—two for the deck extension plus six for the new stairs—placed without disturbing the three existing posts. Full-length band joists of 2×8 redwood tied the new and old structures together. Then extension joists were dropped into joist hangers. Instead of tearing up all the 2×6 decking, I saved money by replacing the few damaged boards and several boards at random to give a look of continuity.

I built a new stairway that led down to the patio (now paved with inexpensive seconds that look and wear as well as full-price bricks). This integrated the family-gathering areas of the

Before and after photos tell the story: Original cramped deck (left) was extended and transformed by imaginative use of inexpensive materials (right).

35

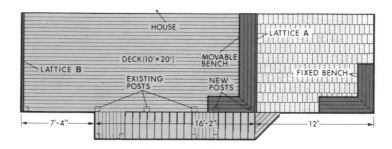

yard. I used landings to make the stairway less steep—and safer for children to use.

To spruce up the deck and increase privacy, I replaced much of the original stick railing with 4-by-8-foot redwood lattice panels. These panels were also used on the landings and to screen the area below the deck. This concealed space makes an excellent storage area for firewood and bulky items that aren't harmed by outdoor exposure. When covered by vines, the panels soften the wood look of the deck and help it blend in with the green of the yard. Finally, I built a movable L-shape bench, which provides flexible deck-side seating.—*Texts by Steve Fikar, Alfred Gran, Elizabeth Strain; all drawings by Gerhard Richter.*

Small rear windows over a steeply sloped yard (see opposite) didn't take advantage of a water-front view. One architect's solution: this spacious bi-level deck with spa, glass-shielded observation post, and cooking area. The handsome fascia doubles as a structural brace. (See ch. 5 for story.)

4 Step-up Deck for Sloping Yards

An angled planter (bottom left) marks the transition from lower deck to platform—it's built into the latter's framing. This is the view to the right as you step out onto the deck; the photo at right bottom shows the left end of the deck, with a trellis for hanging plants. The main deck area (large photo, top) offers generous built-in seating. It's all built of pressure-treated lumber, with a sealer coat.

The young homeowners were happy about their first house—until they walked around back. The builder had never properly regraded the backyard, and its pronounced slope ruled out laying a patio. The house itself was not at its best here, either: a series of setbacks fractured its rear elevation, and, ironically, several back doors offered access to . . . nothing.

A major unifying structure was needed to tame the wild yard. So the couple took their problems to a local Georgia-Pacific Corp. dealer and formulated plans for a bi-level deck that flows around the jogs and beckons family and friends outdoors from nearly every room along the back of the house.

That's the purpose of the lower section, which was spliced directly to the house by means of 2×10 ledger boards lagscrewed into the foundation. Once you've stepped out onto this deck, you can either turn toward the left end, with its trellised barbecue area, or head to the right of the built-in planter and up three steps to an elevated section that features wide backless benches instead of a railing, and even wraps around a clump of existing trees. "For parties, especially," the homeowners report, "the platform is the most popular 'room' in the house. And it's broad enough to take a table and chairs for more formal alfresco dining."

The amount of lumber you'll need depends, of course, on the area you want to cover, but the 663-square-foot deck shown here called for about 950 feet of 2×6s and 650 feet of 2×4s, mainly for decking (where the two widths are alternated). Construction also called for eight 10-foot 4×4s for posts, plus 2×8s, 2×10s, and 2×12s. The total cost for all materials, including 120 joist hangers and 100 pounds of No. 16 hot-dipped galvanized nails, came to less than $2,000. All the lumber was

STEP-UP DECK FOR SLOPING YARDS

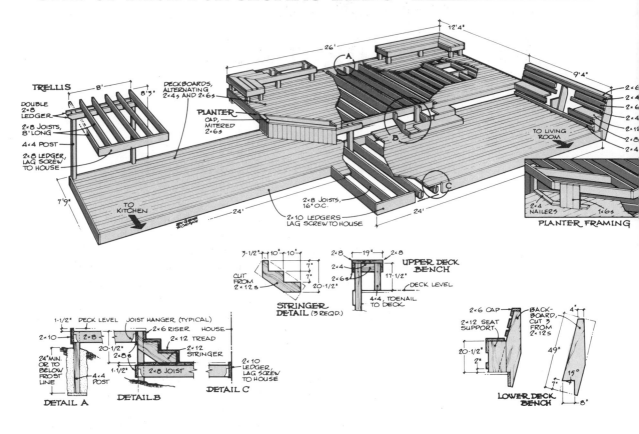

TRELLIS — 8' —

DOUBLE
2×8
LEDGER

2×8 JOISTS,
8' LONG

4×4 POST

2×8 LEDGER,
LAG SCREW
TO HOUSE

7'9"

TO
KITCHEN

24'

DECKBOARDS,
ALTERNATING
2×4s AND 2×6s

PLANTER
CAP,
MITERED
2×6s

8'5"

26'

12'4"

9'4"

TO LIVING
ROOM

2×6
2×4
2×6
2×4
2×12
2×8
2×4

2×8 JOISTS,
16" O.C.

2×10 LEDGERS
LAG SCREW TO HOUSE

24'

PLANTER FRAMING

2×4
NAILERS

1×6s

3-1/2" 10" 10"

CUT
FROM
2×12s

7"
7"

20-1/2"

STRINGER
DETAIL (3 REQD.)

2×8 — 19" — 2×8

2×4

2×6s

17-1/2"

UPPER DECK
BENCH

DECK LEVEL

4×4, TOENAIL
TO DECK

2×6 CAP

2×12 SEAT
SUPPORT

20-1/2"

2"

BACK-
BOARD,
CUT 3
FROM
2×12s

4"

49"

15°

7"

LOWER DECK
BENCH

8"

1-1/2" DECK LEVEL JOIST HANGER (TYPICAL)

2×10

2×8

HOUSE

2×6 RISER

2×12 TREAD

2×12
STRINGER

20-1/2"
2×8s

24" MIN.
OR TO
BELOW
FROST
LINE

4×4
POST

1-1/2"

2×8 JOIST

2×10
LEDGER,
LAG SCREW
TO HOUSE

DETAIL A

DETAIL B

DETAIL C

CCA pressure-treated southern pine. If you choose redwood or cedar instead, your lumber costs will be higher.

Preservative-treated lumber is sold with various levels of retention. For your posts (and any other wood that will be in contact with the ground), ask for a 0.40 level. For above-ground wood, a retention level of 0.25 will suffice.

How you anchor the ledger to the house depends on how it relates to your foundation. Because it's the lower deck that abuts the house, you may have to attach your ledger boards to the masonry. (With higher decks you can often lag-screw ledgers directly into the house framing.) At any rate, you'll want to keep the finished deck surface below the thresholds of all existing or added access doors.

The 2×10 ledgers for the deck shown were attached by removing the house's bottom sheathing board to drill holes into the concrete blocks 2 feet apart; 6-inch lag bolts were driven into lag shields tapped into these holes.

To determine the outer corners, stake out your deck with string tacked to the ends of the ledgers, then dig holes at the post locations—about a foot in diameter and at least 2 feet deep. The homeowners on this project placed a concrete cap block in each hole, stood the post on top, and held the post plumb with staked braces while filling the hole flush with concrete. Be sure to let the concrete set 48 hours before tapping the braces loose.

When all posts are in place, bridge them with 2×10 beams and band joists, outlining the entire lower-deck area. Check all installations with a carpenter's level before attaching them permanently. Nail joist hangers onto opposite inner faces (spaced 16 inches on center); drop 2×8 joists in place and nail them through the hangers. Now, nail the decking atop the joists, alternating 2×4s with 2×6s. All end-to-end butt joints must be centered on a joist, and these joints should be staggered so adjacent joints don't fall on the same joist.

In building the lower-deck bench, with its tall back, alternate 2×4s and 2×6s as shown in the drawing, using a 2×12 for the seat. Use angle-cut 2×12s, nailed to the band joist, to form the vertical back supports.

The 4×4 posts that support the outer corners of the upper deck extend 17½ inches above the deck's surface because they also support the built-in benches. Add 4×4 posts to the planter area and any framing you do around existing trees.

As with the lower deck, once all the outline beams and band joists are in place, install the inner joists and nail on the decking planks. Don't bother trying to cut the final planks in the rows to exact length before installing; instead, let them project raggedly beyond the band joist, and trim them flush with a portable circular saw after all decking is installed.

Assembly of the steps between the two decks is simple (see drawing)—but critical. Because the actual width of the 2×6 riser is 5½ inches and the actual thickness of the 2×12 tread is 1½ inches, the total height of each step will be 7 inches. The supporting stringers can be cut from 2×12s as shown; you'll need three, one at each end and one at the center.

When all construction is complete, you should brush on a water repellent. Or, if you wish to change the greenish tinge of treated wood, let it weather until this effect lessens, then brush on a pigmented repellent of the color you prefer.—*Text by Alfred Lees; drawings by Eugene Thompson.*

5 Elevated Deck with Spa

The view across Long Island Sound to the Connecticut coastline can be magnificent—particularly if you're gazing out, glass of wine in hand, from a second-story heated spa high above the north-shore beaches.

That's just the way a Long Island couple wanted to enjoy their waterfront view—and entertain friends. But there were complications: The backyard was steeply sloped and not private. And the small rear windows of the cottage-cum-Tudor-style home didn't afford much of a view.

The couple sought help from professional architect Jack Hillbrand. His solution? A 675-square-foot elevated deck that features:

- A year-round hot tub.
- A raised, glassed-in sun deck.
- An entertainment area with built-in seating.
- A decorative—but structurally necessary—fascia.
- A cooking area with adjacent built-in countertop.
- French doors that lead from den to deck.

The problems were both structural and aesthetic. The deck, 15 feet above the ground, had to support an elevated cedar-stave spa 6 feet in diameter that, when filled with 630 gallons of water and eight people, would weigh 6,500 pounds. Heavy-duty support was needed from the footings, posts, and beams (see construction drawings). For additional support—and for several other reasons—the architect added a fascia, a horizontal band that acts as a structural diaphragm to brace the deck against racking and twisting tendencies.

Although many deck builders use cross-bracing between posts, that design would have left the deck open—and easily visible from neighboring yards. The fascia ensures privacy while providing the structure with a sense of individuality and offering a visual balance to the house's dominating rear elevation.

See color photo on page 37.

42

Impressive-size deck (above and page 37) has heated spa—protected with rollable cedar-slat top—shielded by observation/sun deck with safety-glass enclosure (right). Built-in seating accommodates sun-hungry guests, and there's a convenient enclosed shower (top). Even grill area (left) features pleasant views. It features a built-in countertop.

43

ELEVATED DECK WITH SPA

6 x 6 POSTS

NORTH ELEVATION

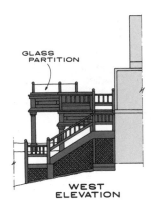

GLASS PARTITION

WEST ELEVATION

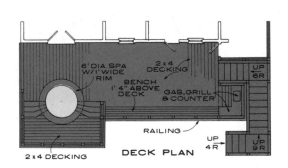

6' DIA. SPA W/1' WIDE RIM

2 x 4 DECKING

BENCH 1' 4" ABOVE DECK

GAS, GRILL & COUNTER

UP 6R

RAILING

UP 4R

UP 9R

2 x 4 DECKING

DECK PLAN

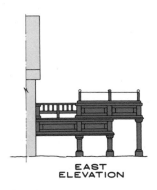

EAST ELEVATION

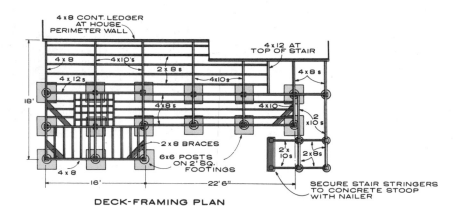

4 x 8 CONT. LEDGER AT HOUSE PERIMETER WALL

4 x 12 AT TOP OF STAIR

4 x 8

4 x 10's

2 x 8 s

4 x 10's

4 x 8 s

4 x 12 s

4 x 8's

4 x 10

2 x 10 s

18'

2 x 8 BRACES

6 x 6 POSTS ON 2' SQ. FOOTINGS

4 x 8

16'

22' 6"

2 x 10 s

2 x 8 s

SECURE STAIR STRINGERS TO CONCRETE STOOP WITH NAILER

DECK-FRAMING PLAN

DETAILS OF DECK

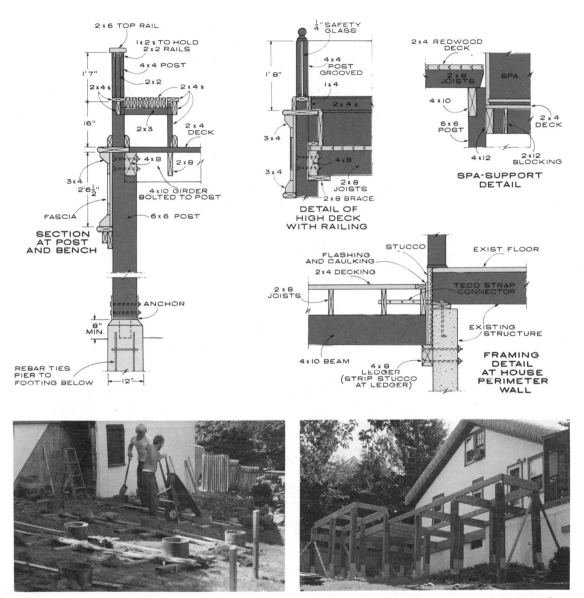

SECTION AT POST AND BENCH

2 x 6 TOP RAIL

1 x 2 s TO HOLD 2 x 2 RAILS

4 x 4 POST

1' 7"

2 x 4 s

2 x 2

2 x 4 s

16"

2 x 3

2 x 4 DECK

4 x 8

2 x 8

3 x 4

2' 6½"

4 x 10 GIRDER BOLTED TO POST

FASCIA

6 x 6 POST

ANCHOR

8" MIN.

REBAR TIES PIER TO FOOTING BELOW

12"

DETAIL OF HIGH DECK WITH RAILING

¼" SAFETY GLASS

4 x 4 POST GROOVED

1 x 4

1' 8"

2 x 4 s

3 x 4

4 x 8

3 x 4

2 x 8 JOISTS

2 x 8 BRACE

SPA-SUPPORT DETAIL

2 x 4 REDWOOD DECK

2 x 8 JOISTS

SPA

4 x 10

6 x 6 POST

2 x 4 DECK

4 x 12

2 x 12 BLOCKING

FRAMING DETAIL AT HOUSE PERIMETER WALL

STUCCO

EXIST. FLOOR

FLASHING AND CAULKING

2 x 4 DECKING

TECO STRAP CONNECTOR

2 x 8 JOISTS

EXISTING STRUCTURE

4 x 10 BEAM

4 x 8 LEDGER (STRIP STUCCO AT LEDGER)

Footings were set three feet below grade: 2½-by-2½-foot footings for under tub, 2-by-2-foot elsewhere, topped with piers (left). Posts were nailed into ¼-inch bent-steel-plate base anchors. The 4 × 8 ledger was fastened to foundation by ¾-inch-diameter bolts. Beams were toenailed to ledger, and joists were strapped to foundation's top plate with 16-gauge steel (right). Seats in posts took beams, secured with ¾-inch bolts (section above left).

The deck runs the full width of the house—another way of integrating the addition with the home's massive rear facade. The deck's length made possible four entrances from the house: the kitchen, the screened porch, the yard, and the den, where elegant French doors replaced a small window. Construction began with the pouring of footings for the installation of the posts: 8 × 8s were used so they could be notched for the beams, and to create a sense of equal scale between deck and house. But 6 × 6 posts, as shown in the drawings, would do the job with less bulk. Major beams are composites of three 2 × 12s at 7-foot centers. For additional support under the spa, a grid of 2 × 12 joists was installed, laid 12 inches on center.

The fascia consists of ¾-inch exterior plywood nailed post to post, framed in beveled 3 × 4s and 1 × 4 trim.

The observation/sun deck increases the sense of spaciousness and adds a distinctive touch. This deck is set three steps above the main deck: That allows comfortable seating on the tub's 12-inch-wide rim. Next, the ¼-inch tempered glazing was installed and secured in quarter-round molding at the base and post extensions. This windscreen deflects gusts over the heads of tub users and allows a clear view of the beach front and water.

The owners planned on using the spa in all seasons, so all exposed plumbing had to be insulated and weatherized. A thermostat was installed under the deck to control the temperature. The gas heater is kept in the garage.

For the stairs, 2 × 12 stringers have 1½-by-1½-inch steel angles to receive treads of three 2 × 4s. Double 2 × 10s support the two landings. Simple wood-lattice screens hide the underside of the stairs and deck. The balusters were 2 × 2s set between 2 × 6 rails. As a decorative touch—and to match the stairs to the windbreak—the newel posts were capped with spherical finials.

Built-in benches provide plenty of seating. The benches, which measure 16 inches high and 20 inches deep, were built from 2 × 4s set on edge, ½-inch apart within a frame of flat-laid 2 × 4s. Bench posts are 4 × 4s along the backs, 2 × 4s in front (see section) with beveled 2 × 4s as base plinths. The deck's top rail, which is built of continuous 2 × 6s with 1 × 2 stops and 2 × 2 balusters, stands about 36 inches high. The deck was finished with Samuel Cabot's Driftwood Gray semitransparent stain.

Finally, because the deck would be used at night, concealed low-voltage lights were installed under the steps and along the underside of the built-in seating.—*Photos by Greg Sharko.*

6 Glass Railing Preserves the View

During my many years as Home Improvement Editor of *Popular Science Monthly*, I worked closely with various national associations of lumber-product manufacturers, alerting them to keep watch for especially original deck designs. Their field reps or member mills often came across local projects of interest, and professional designers would often send snapshots of projects they were particularly proud of to the association headquarters, which would then query me as to whether the project met editorial requirements.

As described in the opening chapter of this section, I even set up a national contest with one of these organizations – California Redwood Assn.—to uncover innovative decks we'd not have heard about otherwise. Our initial contest was such a success, CRA wanted to repeat it. I asked them to find me a deck that dramatically solved a problem, so *Popular Science* could publish it as an example when the repeat contest was announced.

The subject of this chapter was CRA's response. Designer Dana Nadeau of Capistrano Beach, Calif., took advantage of the drawbacks of a problem site—an irregularly shaped plot of steep terrain—to create a deck of several levels and odd angles. This suited the homeowners perfectly: They wanted to add distinction to their 20-year-old Spanish-style tract house and specified that they didn't want a conventional square deck.

But their main concern was preserving their panoramic view of the Pacific Ocean. Because the drop from the deck's outer edge would be severe, a protective railing was essential. Indeed, since the deck would be used for alfresco dining and for sunning after soaking in the spa, an open-banister rail wouldn't do: A solid windbreak was needed. And that would mask the view

Glass railing (above) retains the view yet
provides shelter for the spa. "Before"
view (right) reveals the steep hillside that
the deck reclaims.

48

A view overlooking the stepped-up spa deck.

for anyone seated on the deck or inside the home's sliding glass doors. The solution to these problems was a sturdy railing of easily-cleaned glass panels.

This deck's various levels are differentiated by the patterns in which the nearly 1,400 square feet of 2 × 6 redwood decking is laid, to add visual interest. The lowest level, down two steps from the larger section, projects far over the hillside. The larger section is built at ground level. A third level climbs up behind the Sundance acrylic whirlpool spa, which is flanked by tapered steps that give access to the raised portion from which you step into the spa; this deck also hides the spa's plumbing and electrical service. This commercial model comes with its own redwood skirt, which remains exposed at the front in this installation. The spa was simply set on a ground-level slab and the deck was erected around it. For greater privacy, the rail behind the spa has a redwood lattice screen instead of a glass panel.

Deck planks and the posts and caps for the railing—in fact, all visible lumber—is redwood. Clear and select grades were chosen to be free of knots but to display an interesting pattern of lighter-colored sapwood. The supporting structure of the deck was constructed of pressure-treated Douglas fir.

The projecting lower section is supported on 4 × 4 posts set

49

GLASS RAILING DECK

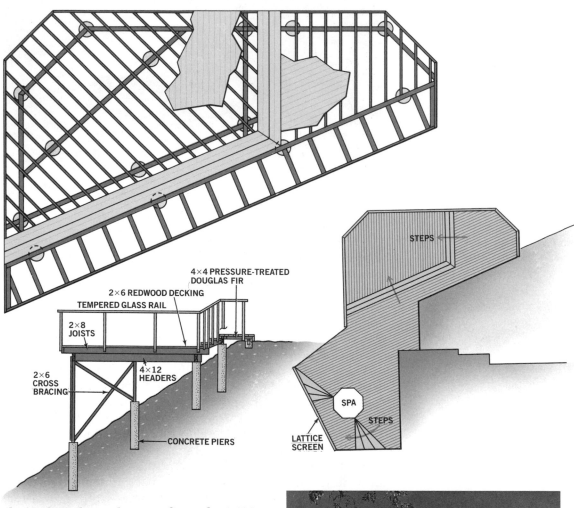

4×4 PRESSURE-TREATED DOUGLAS FIR

2×6 REDWOOD DECKING

TEMPERED GLASS RAIL

2×8 JOISTS

2×6 CROSS BRACING

4×12 HEADERS

CONCRETE PIERS

STEPS

SPA

STEPS

LATTICE SCREEN

Floor plan shows layout of nearly 1,400 square feet of decking. Spa is in sheltered area next to house, while areas for sunning and enjoying the view project over the bank.

Though it appears to float from above, deck is firmly anchored to the hillside when seen from below.

Twelve-inch-diameter concrete footings (poured in Sonotubes) support 4 × 4 posts. Cross-bracing members are 2 × 6s. Vertical supports for glass are double-lag-bolted to deck edge (left). Posts are dadoed to accept glass inserts, as are 2 × 6 top caps (right).

into 12-inch-diameter concrete piers. These piers were poured into Sonotube forms dug 54 inches into the hillside. The posts support 4 × 12 headers, which in turn support 2 × 8 joists nailed into galvanized joist hangers. Then 2 × 6 deck planks are nailed across the joists in various patterns. Long 2 × 6s are also used as cross bracing between support posts, but less-costly fir will suffice here.

The deck railing is 46 inches high. Posts, double-bolted through the headers, are dadoed to take the glass inserts and are capped with 2 × 6 planks of vertical-grain redwood, grooved on their undersides. Sections of vertical redwood slats interrupt the flow of glass to add a pattern and help define the deck areas.

The ground-level section of the deck was laid across 4 × 4 pressure-treated joists that rest atop concrete piers (see section sketch). All redwood was finished with Watco oil-based semi-transparent stain to retain its color.—*Text by Alfred Lees; photos by Mark Becker; drawings by Mario Ferro.*

7 Multi-Level Decks

SPA DECK

When Susie and Peter Stevenson first moved into their seaside home north of San Diego they knew that the side entry area needed work. Access was via a steep asphalt walkway that was slippery when wet. At its end rickety steps climbed to a cramped deck that only termites enjoyed.

"We also wanted to cover those eyesore utility meters at the lower corner," Susie tells me. "And I wanted to add some life by building in planter boxes. And if we could include a Jacuzzi, the kids would be ecstatic."

The final design covered all bases: Angled platforms turn the corner much more invitingly than the old blacktop ramp. And by hinging simple frames of redwood lattice, the meters were hidden, yet kept accessible for reading. Framing out this entry wall also provided concealed storage for potting soil, brooms, and spa chemicals.

A spacious new deck running the length of the kitchen/dining-room wall adds useful space for entertaining, and the steps up to the spa deck create a lot of extra seating.

All construction was knotty garden-grade redwood (the Stevensons specified Construction Heart and Construction Common at the lumberyard). After building was under way, clever devices called Dec-Klips came to my attention, so I had a batch of them shipped to the Stevensons. "We were so pleased with the results," Susie reports, "we almost wanted to tear out the deck boards we'd already face-nailed so we could start over with the Klips." As shown in the sketch below, they're simple devices that solve a multitude of problems: They eliminate unsightly

A flight of landings (bottom right) swings around the back corner of the house to cover an old blacktop walkway. These stairs climb to an upper deck, which, at its far end, has two more steps up to a fenced alcove for the spa. Note at far left in top photo that the fence along the lower deck is topped with glass panels that serve as a windbreak without obscuring the ocean view. A tile-topped buffet counter is attached to the house wall (bottom left), sized to garage a rolling service cart. Other house-wall built-ins include a storage bin for potting supplies (bottom right).

BASIC DECK FRAMING AND BUFFET

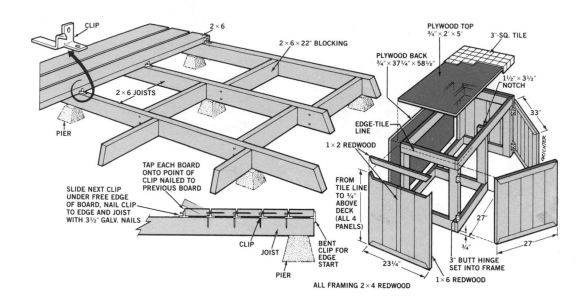

PRODUCT CREDITS

Molded resin furniture includes Cormoran chaise, Diago chairs and tables: Allibert, 1200 Hwy. 27 S., Box 1200, Stanley NC 28164; Lumber: California Redwood Assn., 405 Enfrente Drive, Suite 200, Novato, CA 94949; Spa is "Polara": Jacuzzi Whirlpool Bath, 100 N. Wiget Lane, Walnut Creek CA 94598; Dec-Klips: Philips Manufacturing Co., Ltd., 2306 Madison Ave., Burnaby, British Columbia, Canada V5C 4Z1.

nail heads (and hammer dimples) from the deck surface and automatically space the boards for drainage as you go along. Because you nail into the *side* of each plank, there can be no nail popping later to snag bare feet. And if you ever want to sand down the deck for refinishing, you won't have to set nail heads below the surface to keep them from ripping your sanding belt. "The Klips sped up our whole project," says Susie.

Fence construction was kept simple as well. Vertical 1 × 6 planks, with each joint covered with 1-inch redwood lath for visual interest, were topped with lattice panels and a top rail. Each post was capped with a beveled square cut from a redwood 2 × 6.

POOL DECK

You enter the impressive pool area shown on page 56 through a gated brick archway tucked under a rustic cedar trellis that runs across the back of the house. The entire 1,600-square-foot area beyond is enclosed by a rambling wooden fence topped with redwood lattice that serves as a windbreak

This backyard resort (see Ch. 8) has a built-in lap pool that's easy for the novice to install, using pressure-treated plywood and standard decking procedures.

Complex pattern of levels creates a bleacher effect at far end of pool, with a variety of areas for sunning and seating. There's even a conversation pit—a lower area ringed with several levels of benches.

POOL DECK DETAILS

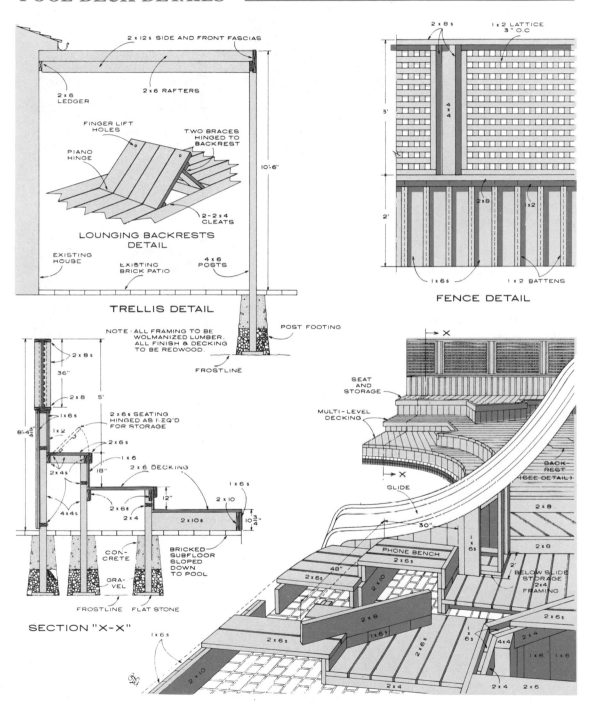

2 x 12s SIDE AND FRONT FASCIAS

2 x 6 RAFTERS

2 x 6 LEDGER

FINGER LIFT HOLES

TWO BRACES HINGED TO BACKREST

PIANO HINGE

2-2 x 4 CLEATS

LOUNGING BACKRESTS DETAIL

10'-6"

EXISTING HOUSE

EXISTING BRICK PATIO

4 x 6 POSTS

TRELLIS DETAIL

2 x 8s

1 x 2 LATTICE 3" O.C

3'

4 x 4

2'

2 x 8

1 x 2

1 x 6s

1 x 2 BATTENS

FENCE DETAIL

2 x 8s

36"

2 x 8

5'

1 x 6s

8'-4 3/4"

1 x 2

2 x 6s SEATING HINGED AS REQ'D FOR STORAGE

2 x 6s

1 x 6

2 x 4s

18"

2 x 6 DECKING

12"

1 x 6s

2 x 10

2 x 6s

4 x 4s

2 x 4

2 x 10s

10 3/4"

CONCRETE

BRICKED SUBFLOOR SLOPED DOWN TO POOL

GRAVEL

FROSTLINE   FLAT STONE

SECTION "X-X"

1 x 6s

2 x 10

NOTE : ALL FRAMING TO BE WOLMANIZED LUMBER. ALL FINISH & DECKING TO BE REDWOOD.

POST FOOTING

FROSTLINE

X

SEAT AND STORAGE

MULTI-LEVEL DECKING

BACK-REST (SEE DETAIL)

X

SLIDE

2 x 8

2 x 8

30"

1 x 6s

2'

BELOW SLIDE STORAGE 2 x 4 FRAMING

PHONE BENCH 2 x 6s

48"

2 x 6s

2 x 10

1 x 6s

2 x 8

2 x 6s

2 x 6s

1 x 6s

1 x 6s

4 x 4

2 x 4

2 x 6s

1 x 6   1 x 6

2 x 4   2 x 6

The rustic trellis along the back of the house is built over the original brick patio. Note the access panel to pool gear, with finger holes.

without impeding gentler breezes. The lattice is framed by 4×4 posts and 2×4 rails top and bottom. The fence consists of 1×6 redwood planks with a redwood 1×2 batten over each joint. Built against it are benches of various heights; sections of the top of the perimeter bench are hinged to give access to storage for pillows and sunning mats.

Sections of the best sunning deck (for early afternoon exposure) are also hinged so they can be raised as back rests. When not in use, the prop brace that holds each four-plank section at a comfortable angle is released and the sections drop flush with the deck surface.

The enclosed area under the foot of the fiberglass slide is a storage compartment for pool chemicals. It also houses a poolside phone, with the adjacent raised trapezoid providing a perch for taking calls with your back to the noise of the pool.

All deck planks are 2×6 redwood. Conventional decking over so large an area would have looked monotonous, so designer Stewart Neely stepped up odd-shaped sections and varied the direction of the planks. The designer was also challenged to preserve two existing sycamore trees. He located the conversation pit beneath one of them, taking advantage of its shade.

The substructure consists of 4×4 pressure-treated posts flanked by 2×6 beams and topped by a complex of joists and blocking that creates the various levels.

Back near the house, deck planks are nailed directly to sleepers laid (24 inches on center) across the existing brick patio. The big trellis is supported by 4×6 cedar posts; 2×6 rafters span the distance between two 2×6 ledgers—one lag-screwed to the house, the other fastened to the rear face of the 2×12 fascia board. There's only one center support post, so this fascia has only one joint, centered on this post.

Where raised deck areas meet the edge of the pool, the ends of the projecting planks are trimmed to the free-form shape with a sabre saw, and short lengths of 2×6 redwood are set in under the trimmed edge. Straight edges of these raised sections are faced with redwood planks, placed on edge.

To avoid corrosion that can stain the deck, be certain that all fasteners are hot-dipped galvanized or stainless steel. Because all levels will see barefoot activity, it's a good idea to round the top corners of all deck planks to minimize splintering. All surfaces got a clear finish.—*Text by Alfred Lees, drawings for spa deck by Gerhart Richter, photos for spa deck by Steven F. Mullensky, photos for pool deck by George Lyons.*

8 Backyard Resort with Built-in Plywood Pool

Jim and JoAnn Lund had a pleasant enough backyard. There was an aging 16-by-32-foot deck off the rear of the house and a barn out on the right side. Most of the rest was taken up by a large garden full of pink and white rhododendrons, azaleas, fruit trees, and flowers of all descriptions.

That was in May. By August the deck had been replaced by a more contemporary-looking one, a lap pool had replaced the garden, and the whole complex had been enclosed by a handsome fence and a trellis that screens out the barn. What's really surprising, however, is that the entire project, excavation excluded, was completed by the Lunds, with the occasional help of two friends, in their spare time over a period of about two months.

The key to this almost magical transformation, besides the homeowners' heroic perseverance, is the pool, which the Lunds obtained as a kit from Sunland Pool Systems. And the secret to the success of the pool lies in the strength and durability of its liner, made from polyvinyl chloride (PVC) film. "No other current polymer compound can be made to withstand the rigors of handling during installation, the effects of exposure to water-treatment chemicals, and the environmental extremes of summer's heat to winter's cold," says Sunland president Peter Stevenson.

It's not only the pool that makes this a terrific project. The offset decking complex and fencing were designed by the landscape architectural firm of Edward Chaffee and Associates in Tacoma, Wash., utilizing construction techniques that let any homeowner—even one inexperienced in construction—feel confident about tackling the installation. Once complete, the backyard resort provides space and privacy for relaxation and sunbathing or elegant outdoor entertaining.

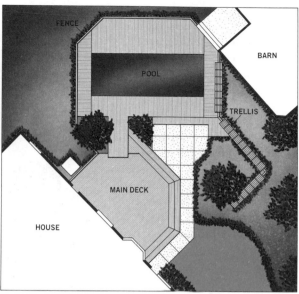

PVC membrane makes an excellent inert lining for pools. With pressure-treated plywood and an innovative liner-track/wood-coping system that lets you carry a wrap-around deck to the pool's edge, you can build a handsome lap pool that has the look of a custom built-in. (This photo is shown in color on page 55.)

The Lunds wanted to install a pool and entertainment area, but they needed to keep costs down.

"There are as many as 50,000 vinyl-liner pools that go in the ground each year," says Rick Kraus, president and owner of Aquaflex Vinyl Engineering, a Sacramento, Calif.-based company that supplies liners to the industry. "Their main attraction is cost savings: a 12-by-32-foot concrete built-in pool will cost you about $11,000. By contrast, a professionally installed vinyl-liner pool with a metal, fiberglass, or wood frame of the same size will cost about $7,000. Do it yourself and you will come in somewhere under $3,500."

Although modern PVC film is the universal material of choice as a pool liner, Kraus told me that the virgin PVC polymer is thermally unstable and must be blended with various ingredients to make it suitable as a swimming-pool liner and competitive with the durability of concrete.

"Unfortunately in the past," says Kraus, "vinyl-liner pools have suffered somewhat from degradation by ultraviolet radiation in sunlight. As with many long-chain polymers, UV radiation can break the bonds between the vinyl chloride monomers that make up the PVC molecule." A recent solution to this problem has been to add an acrylic topcoat to pool liners that effectively blocks the UV radiation and halts PVC breakdown.

Once the Lunds learned about vinyl-lined pools and were

Pool walls are actually simple fence construction: 4×4 posts with 2×6 bracing to which ¾-inch plywood is fastened. The 2×6s are nailed to 2×4 blocking attached to 4×4s. Detail A shows liner treatment: Coping is routed to accept extruded liner track; formed lip of liner snaps into the track. Foam backing protects the liner from the plywood. Corner detail B shows lapped design for extra strength.

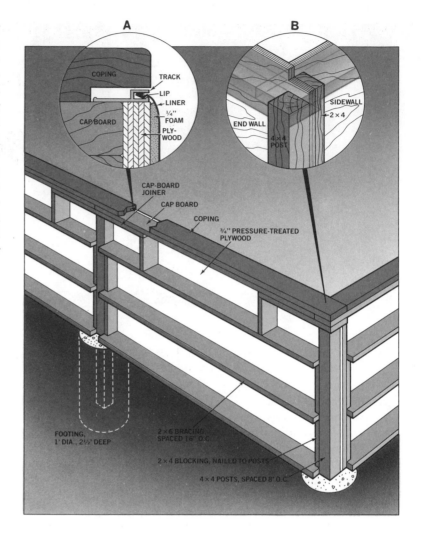

satisfied with the high quality of the product, they decided to install one themselves.

"I'm a furnace repairman," Jim Lund told me, "and I'm pretty good with my hands. But I don't have much construction experience. Pete Stevenson assured me, though, that the pool is so easy to build I wouldn't have any trouble. He was right."

Here's how Stevenson described the procedure to me: "The basic idea behind the pool is to build a fence from which the pool liner can be hung around the inside of a hole. The hole is made about a foot oversize on all sides to allow for wall build-

Sources: American Plywood Assn. (plywood), Box 11700, Tacoma WA 98411; Rubbermaid Inc. (furniture, dinnerware, accessories), 1147 Akron Rd., Wooster OH 44691-0800; Weber-Stephen Products Co. (gas barbecue), 200 E. Daniels Rd., Palatine IL 60067; Western Wood Preserving Co. (Osmose Sunwood pressure-treated lumber), Box 1250, Sumner WA 98390

ing. Fence posts are sunk into holes; 2 × 6 bracing is installed between the posts; and ¾-inch pressure-treated plywood is nailed or screwed onto the inside of the framing. Once the walls are up, ¼-inch packing foam is glued to the inside surface of the plywood to provide both insulation and a smooth surface for the liner. The bottom is then 'iced' with about 2 inches of cushioned insulation (a mixture of a lightening agent such as prolite or vermiculite and concrete).

"Skimmers, outlets, and other fittings are specially made to fit through holes cut in the plywood. Once the extruded top track is nailed around the top of the 'fence,' the lip on the liner can be clipped into the track and adjusted laterally to fit the seams in the corners. Water can be added right away."

Because of the construction of the pool, the Osmose Sunwood pressure-treated decking can be brought to the pool's very edge. All the decking, including the perimeter of the pool, is bordered by doubled 2 × 8s. The decking substructure is formed by 4 × 4 piers set in concrete footings, to which 4 × 8 beams are fastened at intervals no greater than 8 feet on center. In between the beams, 2 × 6 joists are spaced 2 feet on center to support 2 × 4 decking. To preserve the distinctive warm red color of Sunwood lumber, it should be treated with an exterior-grade sealer before weathering can take place.—*Text by Timothy O. Bakke, drawings by Mario Ferro, photo by Strode Photographers.*

TO ORDER POOL KIT AND PLANS

The kit for the 12-by-32-foot pool shown is from Sunland Pool Systems, Box K, Del Mar, Calif. 92014. It costs $1,325 and includes the vinyl liner, liner track, skimmer, return-outlet wall fitting, cartridge-type filter, and one-horsepower filter pump. Custom-size liners are also available.

Complete construction plans, which include directions, photos, materials list, and building-technique illustrations for the pool and deck shown, are available from Stevenson Projects, Box K, Del Mar, Calif. 92014. Cost of the plans is $10. The cost of construction plans is refunded with the purchase of a pool kit.

High-Rise Decks for Above-ground Pools

An above-ground pool may cool off your kids' summers, but it can also leave you worrying about shaky ladders, uninvited swimmers, towels all over the lawn, and wet bodies in the living room.

FREESTANDING POOL AND DECK

One remedy for those cares and woes is this sturdy, safe pool deck, which provides seating for eight swimmers and a swing-up stairway—and can be assembled for around $400.

The deck rests on six pressure-treated 4 × 4s sunk 3 feet down (or below the frost line) and anchored in 14 to 16 inches of concrete. Here are the details:

Attach the 2 × 8 beams to the posts with 3/8-by-3-inch lag bolts and washers. Use a metal hinge bracket for the center crosspiece. I extended the beams past the posts and butted them. Trimming with a router gives the beams a finished look.

Lay the 2 × 4 decking with a 1/8-to-1/4-inch gap between the boards to allow for water runoff. Two 16d nails anchor each board at each beam location. Leave a 1-to-1½-inch clearance between the decking and the top of the pool for installation of solar or winter covers.

The three guardrails are easy to install. The post nearest the stairs provides an upright for the first guardrail. Finish framing with a 4 × 4 bolted to the deck, and attach a 2 × 4 crosspiece. A second guardrail is framed by a post and a seat-back support. A third is disguised as an armrest on the bench seat nearest the stairs.

The stairs are hinged so you can raise them like a drawbridge

Two easy-to-build decks that add safety, storage, and seating to that summertime treat, the above-ground pool—and make it more attractive in the bargain.

FREESTANDING POOL AND DECK

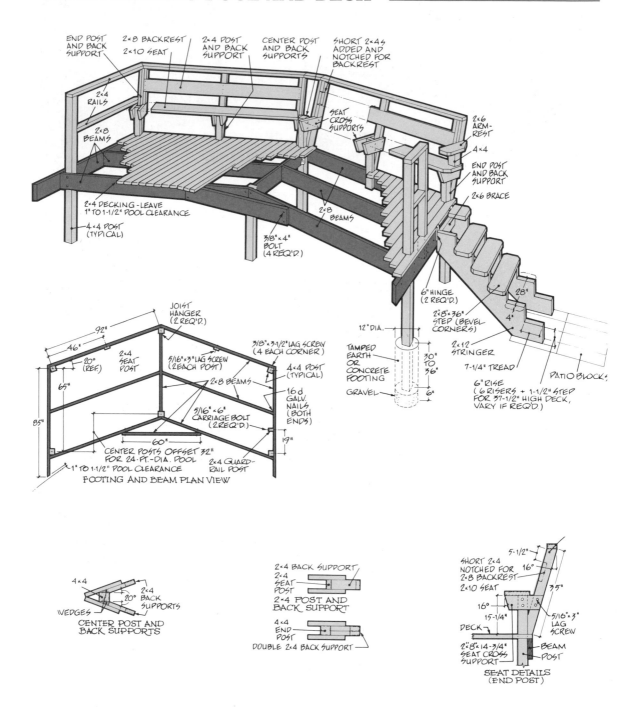

END POST AND BACK SUPPORT

2×8 BACKREST
2×10 SEAT

2×4 POST AND BACK SUPPORT

CENTER POST AND BACK SUPPORTS

SHORT 2×4s ADDED AND NOTCHED FOR BACKREST

2×4 RAILS

SEAT CROSS SUPPORTS

2×6 ARM-REST

4×4

2×8 BEAMS

END POST AND BACK SUPPORT

2×6 BRACE

2×4 DECKING - LEAVE 1" TO 1-1/2" POOL CLEARANCE

2×8 BEAMS

4×4 POST (TYPICAL)

3/8" × 4" BOLT (4 REQ'D.)

6" HINGE (2 REQ'D.)

2"×8"×36" STEP (BEVEL CORNERS)

28"

4"

12" DIA.

TAMPED EARTH OR CONCRETE FOOTING

GRAVEL

30" TO 36"

6"

2"×12" STRINGER

7-1/4" TREAD

PATIO BLOCKS

6" RISE (6 RISERS + 1-1/2" STEP FOR 37-1/2" HIGH DECK, VARY IF REQ'D.)

JOIST HANGER (2 REQ'D.)

92"

46"

20° (REF.)

2×4 SEAT POST

3/8"×3-1/2" LAG SCREW (4 EACH CORNER)

5/16"×3" LAG SCREW (2 EACH POST)

4×4 POST (TYPICAL)

65"

2×8 BEAMS

16d GALV. NAILS (BOTH ENDS)

85"

5/16"×6" CARRIAGE BOLT (2 REQ'D.)

60"

19"

CENTER POSTS OFFSET 32" FOR 24-FT.-DIA. POOL

2×4 GUARD-RAIL POST

1" TO 1-1/2" POOL CLEARANCE

FOOTING AND BEAM PLAN VIEW

4×4

2×4 BACK SUPPORTS

WEDGES

20°

CENTER POST AND BACK SUPPORTS

2×4 BACK SUPPORT

2×4 SEAT POST

2×4 POST AND BACK SUPPORT

4×4 END POST

DOUBLE 2×4 BACK SUPPORT

5-1/2"

SHORT 2×4 NOTCHED FOR 2×8 BACKREST

16°

2×10 SEAT

35"

16°

15-1/4"

DECK

5/16"×3" LAG SCREW

2"×8"×14-3/4" SEAT CROSS SUPPORT

BEAM

POST

SEAT DETAILS (END POST)

66

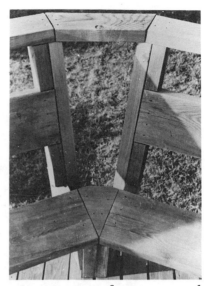

To simplify construction, posts serve as supports for wraparound benches. Cut a niche in the 4 × 4 uprights for 2 × 8 backrests, and nail to deck. Seats are 2 × 8s nailed to blocks.

to block off entry to the pool. I used a hook and eye to hold the stairs up, but you may prefer a chain and padlock. Rest the stairs on patio blocks or pour a concrete pad.

Pool ladders are two 4-foot ladders connected by a platform. For stability, remove one of the ladders and bracket the platform to the beam.

The area under the deck is an ideal spot for hanging hoses, vacuums and skimmers. You may also want to use this space to hide the filter system and pump.

BACKDOOR DECK IS BRIDGE TO POOL

Is your above-ground pool an island unto itself? Does it stick out in your backyard like a sore thumb? Here's a deck that connects house and pool, increases storage space, and holds a clan of tanners and bathers.

Start building the deck by anchoring the 4 × 4 pressure-treated cedar posts into metal bases on top of concrete footings. My plans called for a deck 16 by 22 feet, so I sank 9 holes

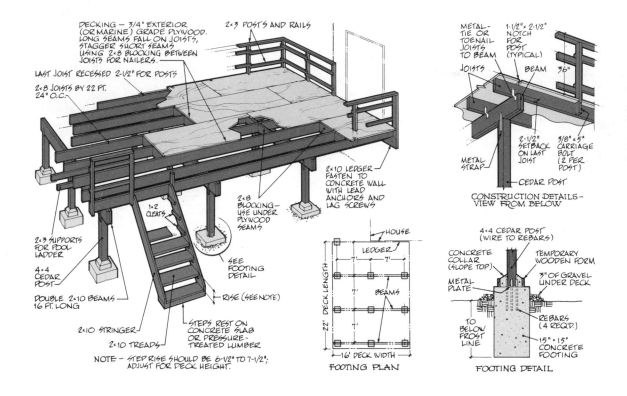

DECKING — 3/4" EXTERIOR (OR MARINE) GRADE PLYWOOD. LONG SEAMS FALL ON JOISTS, STAGGER SHORT SEAMS USING 2×8 BLOCKING BETWEEN JOISTS FOR NAILERS.

LAST JOIST RECESSED 2-1/2" FOR POSTS

2×8 JOISTS BY 22 FT. 24" O.C.

2×3 POSTS AND RAILS

2×10 LEDGER FASTEN TO CONCRETE WALL WITH LEAD ANCHORS AND LAG SCREWS

2×8 BLOCKING - USE UNDER PLYWOOD SEAMS

1×2 CLEATS

2×3 SUPPORTS FOR POOL LADDER

4×4 CEDAR POST

DOUBLE 2×10 BEAMS 16 FT. LONG

2×10 STRINGER

2×10 TREADS

SEE FOOTING DETAIL

RISE (SEE NOTE)

STEPS REST ON CONCRETE SLAB OR PRESSURE-TREATED LUMBER

NOTE – STEP RISE SHOULD BE 6-1/2" TO 7-1/2"; ADJUST FOR DECK HEIGHT.

METAL TIE OR TOENAIL JOISTS TO BEAM

1-1/2" × 2-1/2" NOTCH FOR POST (TYPICAL)

JOISTS

BEAM

36"

METAL STRAP

2-1/2" SETBACK ON LAST JOIST

3/8" × 5" CARRIAGE BOLT (2 PER POST)

CEDAR POST

CONSTRUCTION DETAILS - VIEW FROM BELOW

HOUSE

LEDGER

BEAMS

22' DECK LENGTH

7' 7'

7'

7'

16' DECK WIDTH

FOOTING PLAN

4×4 CEDAR POST (WIRE TO REBARS)

CONCRETE COLLAR (SLOPE TOP)

METAL PLATE

TEMPORARY WOODEN FORM

3" OF GRAVEL UNDER DECK

TO BELOW FROST LINE

REBARS (4 REQ'D.)

15" × 15" CONCRETE FOOTING

FOOTING DETAIL

in rows of 3, with the posts 7 feet apart along the length and 5 feet apart along the width. A tenth post supports the ledger where it extends past the house.

I used lead shields and 3/8-by-4-inch lag bolts to attach the 2×10 ledger to the foundation. Many decks this high can just be fastened to the box beam or sill plate, so won't require drilling into concrete.

Install the 2×10 deck beams parallel to the ledger. I chose to nail 2 beams together, attaching them to the post with a sheet-metal anchor. A more common approach is to run one beam on each side of the post and bolt them through.

Next, attach the 2×8 joists to the beams with metal joist hangers and 1-inch roofing nails. Then bolt the 2×3 railing uprights to the joists. This is a good time to lay a surface under

Kitchen window was removed and opening enlarged to take sliding glass doors for easy access and better view. Guardrails are 2 × 3s bolted to joists, with staggered 2 × 3 crosspieces.

the deck. I recommend a 3-inch bed of gravel to prevent puddling, which deters mosquito and weed growth.

Redwood boards often are used for decks, but I decided to go with ¾-inch marine-grade plywood. (If it's good enough for boats, it's good enough for pool decks.) Because plywood comes in 4-by-8 foot sheets, spacing for runoff isn't possible. However, you can lay the plywood so that it slopes 1 inch every 7 feet or so away from the house. To facilitate drainage I drilled ¼-inch-diameter holes every 12 inches.

To further enhance the yard, I added a patio around the stairs. It also prevents dirt from being tracked up to the deck and into the pool.—*Texts by Vernon J. Sterba and Tony Laurie, drawings by Eugene Thompson.*

10 Simple Elegance: Low or High

LOW

Alfresco entertaining in the evening is the pattern at the northern Illinois home of Marc and Barb Posner—and they had the setting for it: Their spacious yard backed onto a wooded area. But their builder had provided only a concrete stoop outside the back door from the kitchen. And the sliding patio door from the living room was an awkward step down to bare lawn. The grass stayed damp after a rain, and there was no adequate outdoor lighting; guests moved indoors at dusk.

The Posners took their problem to Wickes Lumber's local building-supply center. There they found a batch of well-designed deck plans, one of which was quickly modified to fit their needs—the deck flows around to fill the setback in their back wall, connecting the two rear doors. They chose Deck Plank Wolmanized lumber—pressure-treated planks in lengths of 8 to 16 feet. This $5/4 \times 6$ decking is lighter and cheaper than nominal 2-inch stock. The latter's actual thickness is $1\frac{1}{2}$ inches against Deck Plank's $1\frac{1}{4}$. And the Posners found that the rounded edges lent themselves to built-in benches and steps, as well.

The deck frame rests on a total of 11 concrete piers. Packaged concrete was mixed and shoveled into the holes. As it reached the top, a 2-foot length of 6-inch-diameter galvanized stove pipe was inserted and adjusted to the proper height for each pier; the remaining mix was shoveled into the pipes, which became permanent forms.

The tops of these piers must be flat and at proper heights, because the frame of the deck simply rests on them, without anchors. The deck is actually fastened only to the house walls.

The railing the Posners chose is a modification of the standard precut component system available from Wickes. The final

THE LOW DECK

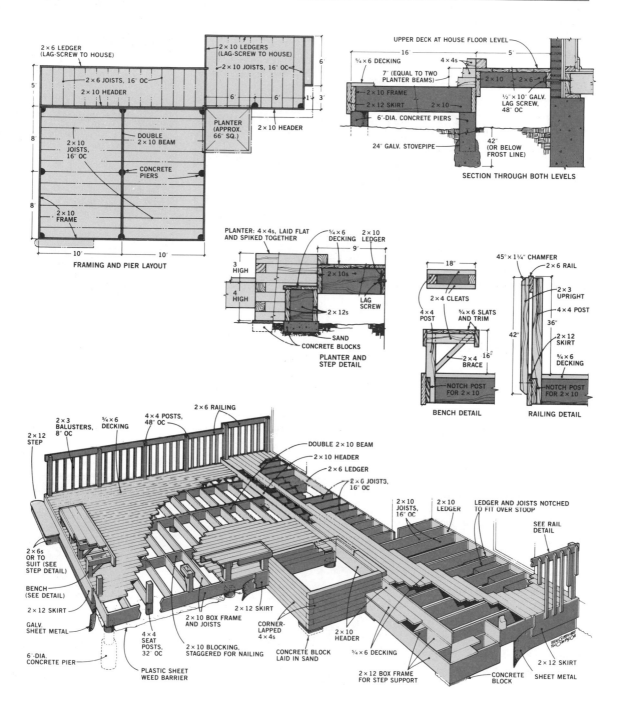

2×6 LEDGER
(LAG-SCREW TO HOUSE)

2×10 LEDGERS
(LAG-SCREW TO HOUSE)

2×6 JOISTS, 16" OC

2×10 JOISTS, 16" OC

2×10 HEADER

6'

5'

6'

6'

1'

3'

PLANTER
(APPROX.
66" SQ.)

2×10 HEADER

8'

2×10
JOISTS,
16" OC

DOUBLE
2×10 BEAM

CONCRETE
PIERS

8'

2×10
FRAME

10'   10'

FRAMING AND PIER LAYOUT

UPPER DECK AT HOUSE FLOOR LEVEL

16'   5'

⅝×6 DECKING   4×4s

7" (EQUAL TO TWO
PLANTER BEAMS)

2×10   2×6

2×10 FRAME

2×12 SKIRT   2×10

½"×10" GALV.
LAG SCREW,
48" OC

6"-DIA. CONCRETE PIERS

24" GALV. STOVEPIPE

42"
(OR BELOW
FROST LINE)

SECTION THROUGH BOTH LEVELS

PLANTER: 4×4s, LAID FLAT
AND SPIKED TOGETHER

⅝×6
DECKING

2×10
LEDGER

9'

3
HIGH

2×10s

4
HIGH

2×12s

LAG
SCREW

SAND

CONCRETE BLOCKS

PLANTER AND
STEP DETAIL

18"

2×4 CLEATS

4×4
POST

⅝×6 SLATS
AND TRIM

2×4
BRACE

16"

BENCH DETAIL

45°×1¼" CHAMFER

2×6 RAIL

2×3
UPRIGHT

4×4 POST

36"

42"

2×12
SKIRT

⅝×6
DECKING

NOTCH POST
FOR 2×10

RAILING DETAIL

2×3
BALUSTERS,
8" OC

⅝×6
DECKING

4×4 POSTS,
48" OC

2×6 RAILING

2×12
STEP

DOUBLE 2×10 BEAM

2×10 HEADER

2×6 LEDGER

2×6 JOISTS,
16" OC

2×10
JOISTS,
16" OC

2×10
LEDGER

LEDGER AND JOISTS NOTCHED
TO FIT OVER STOOP

SEE RAIL
DETAIL

2×6s
OR TO
SUIT (SEE
STEP DETAIL)

BENCH
(SEE DETAIL)

2×12 SKIRT

GALV.
SHEET METAL

6"-DIA.
CONCRETE PIER

4×4
SEAT
POSTS,
32" OC

PLASTIC SHEET
WEED BARRIER

2×10 BOX FRAME
AND JOISTS

2×10 BLOCKING,
STAGGERED FOR NAILING

2×12 SKIRT

CORNER-
LAPPED
4×4s

CONCRETE BLOCK
LAID IN SAND

2×10
HEADER

⅝×6 DECKING

2×12 BOX FRAME
FOR STEP SUPPORT

CONCRETE
BLOCK

2×12 SKIRT

SHEET METAL

71

Once the perimeter of the deck was staked out, holes for 11 concrete piers were drilled with a power auger to below frost line (left).

Ledgers are the only part of the support frame to be anchored. Holes were drilled at 4 foot intervals through joints in the brick veneer so lag screws could be driven into the house's band joist (right).

Rather than break up existing concrete stoop, 2 × 10s used for both ledger and joists were notched over it; this still keeps the top of the deck below the sill.

Deck Plank lumber is nailed on, butted snug so that, as it seasons, ⅛ inch cracks will open for drainage. Planks notch around posts that are bolted through the frame.

To keep nesting animals out, aluminum flashing is nailed along perimeter joists, then masked with skirt boards.

Planter section is made of lap-corner 4 × 4s down to ground level. After they're spiked together, edges of top units are rounded with a router (right) to match edge treatment of Deck Plank lumber; then the pit is filled.

The Posner's low-level deck hugs the setback in their back wall
providing access to the deck from both of their rear doors.

One feature that gives this second-story deck distinction is the oblique step-up between activity levels, shown on next page. It lets you vary the plank pattern and build in a pair of planters.

touches were Malibu low-voltage lights installed around the perimeter, and the two groupings of Sanibel patio furniture from Samsonite.

HIGH

The access to their steeply sloping backyard was all wrong. As Rick and Sandy Voorhees bought it, the house made them step out onto a precarious perch of a platform at the head of a long stair that descended—incredibly—in the wrong direction: The garage, tucked under the kitchen, is at the end of a steep driveway off to the *left* in the photo on the facing page; but the old stairway led off *right* to a blind corner of the yard, forcing the homeowners to about-face on its base slab.

The yard itself, however, was a glory, surrounded by hardwood forest. So the Voorhees called on New Jersey contractor Mike McNally to create a deck worthy of their view. The design that resulted has transformed their modest home, and the Voorhees family now spends most of the year enjoying the beautiful site. Even the view from inside has been enhanced: A puny

rear window to the left of the door was replaced with a sliding patio door that draws the outdoors in, year round. As a bonus, it offers access to the deck from the dining room as well as through the old door from the kitchen.

All construction was handled by two workers. A great difference between a ground-level deck and an elevated one is that the latter doesn't rest directly on concrete piers but is supported by posts (usually, as here, 4×4s). In both cases, work must start with a staking out of the deck on the ground, using the house wall as a base line. But with an elevated deck, the positioning of the piers—poured flush with ground level or just slightly above—is more critical. McNally always uses metal post bases. These are fastened to each pier with an anchor bolt, set into the concrete after the pour. The best type has a metal platform that keeps the post from direct contact with the concrete to spare the porous butt from perpetual dampness. McNally poured nine piers (in Sonotube forms set in holes dug down to the frost line), later adding a pier-footed pad for the stair stringers to rest on.

At the right end of the deck, four joists extend an extra 4 feet

Soaring cantilever of initial framing (right) will establish exact lengths to cut support posts that show in the second photo and the drawing (next page). Both deck levels are anchored to the house by ledgers lag-screwed to existing framing. Scars on the wall show position of old stoop and stairway, removed for new construction.

THE HIGH DECK

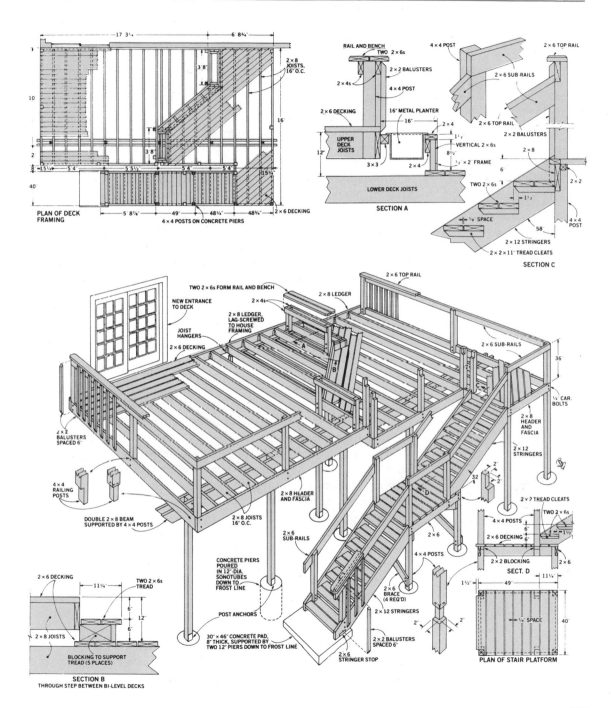

PLAN OF DECK FRAMING
4 × 4 POSTS ON CONCRETE PIERS

2 × 8 JOISTS, 16" O.C.

SECTION A

RAIL AND BENCH
TWO 2 × 6s
2 × 2 BALUSTERS
2 × 4s
4 × 4 POST
2 × 6 DECKING
16" METAL PLANTER
UPPER DECK JOISTS
VERTICAL 2 × 6s
3 × 3
2 × 4
½" × 2" FRAME
TWO 2 × 6s
LOWER DECK JOISTS

4 × 4 POST
2 × 6 TOP RAIL
2 × 6 SUB-RAILS
2 × 6 TOP RAIL
2 × 2 BALUSTERS
2 × 8
2 × 2
4 × 4 POST
⅛" SPACE
2 × 12 STRINGERS
2 × 2 × 11" TREAD CLEATS
58

SECTION C

TWO 2 × 6s FORM RAIL AND BENCH
NEW ENTRANCE TO DECK
2 × 8 LEDGER
2 × 4s
2 × 8 LEDGER, LAG-SCREWED TO HOUSE FRAMING
JOIST HANGERS
2 × 6 DECKING
2 × 6 TOP RAIL
2 × 8 LEDGER
2 × 6 SUB-RAILS
36"
¼" CAR. BOLTS
2 × 8 HEADER AND FASCIA
2 × 12 STRINGERS
2 × 2 BALUSTERS SPACED 6"
4 × 4 RAILING POSTS
DOUBLE 2 × 8 BEAM SUPPORTED BY 4 × 4 POSTS
2 × 8 JOISTS 16" O.C.
2 × 6 SUB-RAILS
2 × 8 HEADER AND FASCIA
2 × 6
4 × 4 POSTS
2 × 2 TREAD CLEATS
4 × 4 POSTS
TWO 2 × 6s
2 × 6 DECKING
2 × 2 BLOCKING
2 × 6
32
2"
2"

SECT. D

CONCRETE PIERS POURED IN 12"-DIA. SONOTUBES DOWN TO FROST LINE
POST ANCHORS
30" × 46" CONCRETE PAD, 8" THICK, SUPPORTED BY TWO 12" PIERS DOWN TO FROST LINE
2 × 6 BRACE (4 REQ'D)
2 × 12 STRINGERS
2 × 6 STRINGER STOP
2 × 2 BALUSTERS SPACED 6"

2 × 6 DECKING
TWO 2 × 6s TREAD
11¼"
6"
6"
12"
2 × 8 JOISTS
BLOCKING TO SUPPORT TREAD (5 PLACES)

SECTION B
THROUGH STEP BETWEEN BI-LEVEL DECKS

1½"
49
11¼"
¼" SPACE
40"

PLAN OF STAIR PLATFORM

Another advantage of metal post bases is that they permit some adjustment, so if you position your poured footings a bit out of line, you can shift the location of the post on the pier enough to keep it plumb with the overhead framing it ties into. Note in McNally's initial construction photo that he and his helper raised two post-and-beam assemblies first, holding them erect with staked props while cantilevering the 2 × 8 joists out from the house ledger atop the double beams. So it's essential that ledgers be well anchored to the house frame or foundation, and that they be absolutely level. For this bi-level deck, ledgers are set at two different heights, with an overlap at the center. Metal joist hangers are nailed to the ledger on 16-inch centers, for the joists to drop into.

to create a platform from which the steps descend. Since the vertical drop from lower deck level to the ground was 8½ feet, McNally felt a continuous run would have been tiring—both to the legs and to the eye. So he constructed a platform about halfway down. This allows a welcome pause while ascending, and adds to the architectural design.

This platform is nothing more than a mini-deck placed in alignment with the staircase. McNally likes to keep the tread-rise ratio as close to 12/6 as possible in an outdoor stair. This meant the use of two 2 × 6 planks for each tread.

Of course, all lumber used in construction was pressure-treated—this should be standard for all deck projects, unless you're using redwood or cedar. For the decking itself, McNally spaced the 2 × 6 planks ⅛-inch apart. "Natural shrinkage will increase the gap," he says, "but not excessively."

The posts that support the deck railing are notched and bolted to the deck's support frame, as detailed below. They're also rabbeted at the top to take the sub-rail. (Note that the rail is an assembly of two 2 × 6s joined to form a T.) The balusters are 2 × 2s trimmed at a 45-degree angle at both ends and nailed in place, spaced 6 inches apart. To avoid corrosion stains, hot-dipped galvanized fasteners were used throughout.

Planters fill the voids to either side of the steps between deck levels. These boxes were created by nailing pressure-treated 1 × 4s to a 2 × 4 frame. When assembly was complete, careful inside measurements were taken so metal inserts could be made at a sheet-metal shop.

Once all decking was laid, attention turned to replacing that small window with a patio-type glass door. Since this was a bearing wall, temporary support was required while the old window was removed and a beefed-up header was installed so that a wider opening could be cut—the rough opening specified by the door manufacturer.

When opening any wall, you must look for runs of electric wires, water lines, or heating ducts. The house shown had both electric and heating lines passing beneath the old window and into the kitchen. These runs had to be rerouted back down to the basement, across, and up to the kitchen. If you're not comfortable with such rerouting, call in professional help; but in any case, cut with caution and only after a thorough check.

Once the new header was in place, the door was inserted from the outside, insulation was stuffed in the cracks, and casing was applied.—*Text by Alfred Lees, drawings by Eugene Thompson, photos by Michael Kelly and Gregg Sharko.*

11 L-Shaped Patio Deck

The rear entry to my kitchen led to a patio adjoining the garage. Trouble was, no one used the patio—it was cramped, unattractive, and run down. But I no longer shudder when someone asks to see my backyard. In fact, I volunteer to show them since I've added a dramatic L-shaped patio deck that allows easy access to the garage, enhances the shrubs along the rear of my house, and, most importantly, adds to the living area of my home. What I like to boast about most, however, is that the project was inexpensive to build.

The new deck gives me a spacious landing at the back door plus plenty of room for outdoor entertaining and storage for barbecue equipment. The entire project was built with Georgia-Pacific pressure-treated lumber, an economical product that is both insect and decay resistant. Its natural finish will gradually weather—it requires no stain or oil treatment for preservation. The warm brown tone fades to a soft, silvery sheen but retains its durability and decay resistance.

The upper level of the deck (about 10 feet square with a diagonal corner) has a built-in bench and rail along the perimeter. It's a perfect place to remove muddy boots or for a chat on a warm evening. A wide step leads to a larger 12-by-20-foot main deck, which is detached from the house and framed at the rear by plants. Beams for the upper deck rest on 4×4 posts set on a concrete slab. (The slab is the old patio. Because it was already in place, I didn't have to contract for costly concrete work.) There are 2×6 ledgers, to which the upper-deck joists are attached, on two sides of the house.

The lower deck is supported on 12-by-12-inch concrete piers. The 4×8 deck beams, which run parallel to the house, are spaced on 3-foot centers and the 2×6 joists on 2-foot centers. All the 2×4 decking is secured with galvanized nails. The deck

L-SHAPED DECK

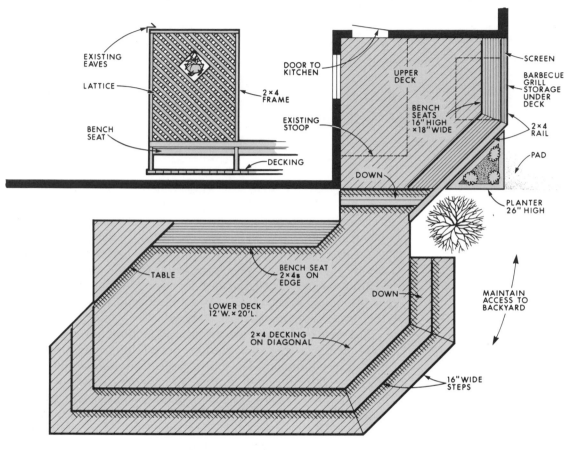

EXISTING EAVES

LATTICE

BENCH SEAT

2 × 4 FRAME

DOOR TO KITCHEN

EXISTING STOOP

DECKING

UPPER DECK

BENCH SEATS 16" HIGH ×18" WIDE

DOWN

SCREEN

BARBECUE GRILL STORAGE UNDER DECK

2 × 4 RAIL

PAD

PLANTER 26" HIGH

TABLE

BENCH SEAT 2 × 4s ON EDGE

DOWN

LOWER DECK 12' W. × 20' L.

2 × 4 DECKING ON DIAGONAL

MAINTAIN ACCESS TO BACKYARD

16" WIDE STEPS

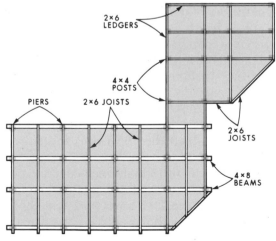

2 × 6 LEDGERS

4 × 4 POSTS

PIERS

2 × 6 JOISTS

2 × 6 JOISTS

4 × 8 BEAMS

Materials needed for the patio deck include: pressure-treated lumber, cedar lattice, galvanized nails, joist hangers, hardware, concrete (for piers), exterior-grade plywood, and sheet metal.

80

A seldom-used stoop and patio at the back of the author's house (right) was replaced by a large two-level deck that wraps around the rear (above).

The 4×8 beams for the lower deck rest on concrete piers and are spaced on three-foot centers (1). The deck's 2×6 joists rest on the beams and are spaced on 24-inch centers. The upper deck is attached to the house with 2×6 ledgers (2). It rests on 4×4 posts set directly on the old patio.

The stairs at the perimeter of the lower deck as well as those bridging the upper and lower decks are set on eight-inch concrete piers (3). The 2×4 decking on the stairs and the main levels was installed diagonally for a striking contrast to the lines of the home (4).

The bench on the lower deck is supported on 2×4 leg assemblies (5) and covered with 2×4s on edge. The table adjoining the bench is framed with 2×4s and surfaced with 2×4s laid flat. The triangular planter box is started using 2×4 scrap (6).

82

boards are spaced apart (approximately the width of a 16-penny nail) to allow for expansion and drainage. All joist hangers and lag and carriage bolts are galvanized.

By angling corners, steps, and benches and laying decking on the bias, I was able to subtly contrast the straight lines of my house. I specified 18-foot lengths of 2 × 4s to avoid seams from joints in the decking.

The benches on both decks were made with 2 × 4s set on edge to contrast with the flat 2 × 4 surface of the deck. The bench supports are framed with three 2 × 4 blocks and a 2 × 4 crosspiece for support. The benches are 16 inches high and 18 inches wide. A triangular table built at the same height as the lower bench and at the corner is covered with 2 × 4s installed on the diagonal (and flat) to match the deck.

I made the planter boxes using scrap lumber from the deck—this helped to tie the area together visually. A large 26-inch-high triangular planter adjoins the upper deck and holds shrubs and annual flowers. There is also a rectangular planter adjacent to the garage door. Rabbeted joints add strength to the planters—the large one was reinforced with 2 × 4 bracing inside to prevent expansion.

Two 16-inch-wide steps, running the perimeter of the lower deck, lead to the ground level. The steps rest on 8-inch piers. The 2 × 6 step framing is surfaced with 2 × 4s installed diagonally to match the deck surfaces.

I also added a decorative lattice screen, built with a 2 × 4 frame, to help screen the garage area from view. A hanging plant makes it a colorful focal point. I can easily take out the screen for winter storage if I want.

I built a storage area beneath the upper deck for stashing barbecue gear, making use of what would have otherwise been wasted space beneath the rail and benches. It's a 3-sided box of exterior-grade CDX plywood that is built on a 2 × 4 frame and covered with sheet metal to keep water out. The box slides under the upper deck. A lattice screen mounted with metal clasps for quick removal hides the equipment from sight.—*Text by Cathy Howard, deck designed and landscaped by Linda Engstrom, drawings by Gerhard Richter.*

12 Four Ways to Add a Patio Deck

BUILD A BARBECUE DECK

Sliding doors to nowhere were a ludicrous feature of this new house in a Chicago suburb. Actually, the doors did lead somewhere: They gave onto a step to the sodded (and sometimes sodden) backyard. But the whole setup looked unfinished—an overdramatic exit to a nondescript space.

Many new homes have such an incongruous layout. The builder assumes that the homeowner will add a concrete patio. But these owners wanted a self-draining cook space for use even after summer storms.

A similar barbecue deck could be added to any house with a ground-level exit (or even a picture window that could be converted to a door). The builder of this deck followed the basic guides outlined in "How to Build a Deck" ($1 from Koppers Co., 1900 Koppers Bldg., Pittsburgh, Pa. 15219). All construction was of Wolmanized lumber.

To begin the barbecue deck, the builder outlined the area with stakes, then dug out the sod. Next he made a jig to mark posthole positions. The builder wanted the posts to be 9 feet from the house wall, so he marked off that distance on two 12-foot planks. Then he nailed another plank across the two 9-foot marks. Butting this reclining "goal post" up against the house, the builder used the crosspiece as a hole-marking guide. He dug four 42-inch-deep postholes, and tamped down a 6-inch layer of gravel in each.

Next he laid a plastic sheet over the de-sodded area, anchoring it along the house with gravel and slitting it over each post-

Clutter-free cook space (above) keeps deck open for entertaining. Strategically placed Charm-glow bug killer protects food area. Handsome angled serving counter (below) is three 2 × 4's supported by braces attached to shed and railing.

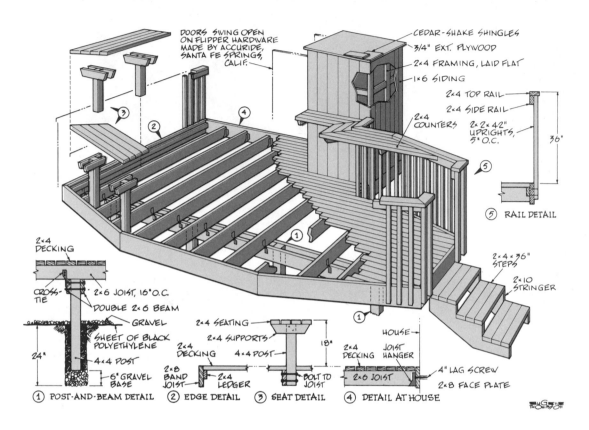

DOORS SWING OPEN ON FLIPPER HARDWARE MADE BY ACCURIDE, SANTA FE SPRINGS, CALIF.

CEDAR-SHAKE SHINGLES
3/4" EXT. PLYWOOD
2×4 FRAMING, LAID FLAT
1×6 SIDING

2×4 TOP RAIL
2×4 SIDE RAIL
2×4 COUNTERS
2×2×42" UPRIGHTS, 5" O.C.

36"

⑤ RAIL DETAIL

③ ④

2×4 DECKING

② ①

2×6 JOIST, 16" O.C.

CROSS-TIE
DOUBLE 2×6 BEAM
GRAVEL
SHEET OF BLACK POLYETHYLENE
24"
4×4 POST
6" GRAVEL BASE

① POST-AND-BEAM DETAIL

2×4 SEATING
2×4 SUPPORTS
2×4 DECKING
4×4 POST
2×8 BAND JOIST
2×4 LEDGER
BOLT TO JOIST
18"

② EDGE DETAIL

③ SEAT DETAIL

2×4×36" STEPS
2×10 STRINGER

HOUSE
2×4 DECKING
JOIST HANGER
2×6 JOIST
4" LAG SCREW
2×8 FACE PLATE

④ DETAIL AT HOUSE

Custom cook deck starts with a simply framed understructure—joists suspended from a house-mounted faceplate and supported on posts with a double beam. Gravel beneath deck anchors a sheet of polyethylene that inhibits weed growth.

Barbecue-grill hideaway (right) has a frame of 2 × 4 studs (left) wrapped with 1 × 6 planks. Shed's slide-away doors ride in a track, and pull out to swing shut. Since the Charmglow Avanti grill shown doesn't need weather protection, the shed's job is to clear the decks for entertaining once the cooking's done. The enclosure also makes the grill handy for year-round barbecues: Open doors can provide a windbreak for "backdoor cooking" on crisp days. (Don't grill inside shed, though.) Enclosure is well ventilated—any propane that leaks during storage of the grill would escape through deck cracks.

Measuring jig (above) looks like a toppled goal post, but was a uniquely simple solution to aligning deck post holes. The four beam posts are quite sufficient to support deck's weight, but builder let one of bench legs pass through deck for extra support at corner.

hole. Folding this outer edge back, he now set four 8-foot 4 × 4s in place. Once these posts were firmly backfilled, he stretched a level line across them and trimmed the tops even at the desired height. After unfolding the plastic cover and spreading gravel over it, he fastened a 16-foot-long support beam across these posts, flush with their trimmed tops. The beam is a pair of 2 × 6s tacked to the sides of the posts so the assembly can be drilled for two ⅜-inch carriage bolts, 8 inches long, at each post.

A 2 × 8 faceplate was fastened to the house wall with 4-inch lag bolts driven into masonry anchors set into the concrete foundation. The same size lumber frames the deck outline as shown, before the 2 × 6 joists are carefully cut to fit within this frame. These are 16 inches on center and hung wherever possible in galvanized joist hangers. Note that the joists are hung flush with the bottom of the outer frame so the deck boards will set flush with the *top* of this frame. Galvanized crossties stabilize each joist where it crosses the double beam.

Before laying the decking, the builder bolted bench legs to the joists. He positioned these 23-inch 4 × 4s so the bench echoes the deck angles. Perpendicular to the top of each leg, he bolted a pair of 15-inch 2×4s to support the bench seat.

The 2×4 deck planks were notched out to fit around the bench supports. Four 2×4s spaced ½-inch apart finished the bench seat. Railing uprights are 3-foot 2×2s spaced 5 inches on center; top and side rails are 2×4s.

Finally, the builder added the special features that make this deck a convenient cook space—the grill enclosure and the railing-mounted serving counter (see photos)—*Text by Susan Renner-Smith, drawings by Eugene Thompson.*

CAMOUFLAGE A CONCRETE SLAB

See color photo on page 91.

The aging concrete patio was ugly—and unused. Rain left pools on its cracked, uneven surface. Bright sun bathed it in an unpleasant glare.

Transforming the slab to a handsome, quick-draining deck took less time and money than you'd expect. The reason? The slab serves as the deck's understructure. This cuts costs for framing lumber. And erecting the understructure is usually the most complex and time-consuming part of deck building (see preceding story).

By contrast, two simple steps convert almost any concrete-slab patio into a deck. The first step: Attach stringers to the concrete. Since the slab supports these undertimbers, the cheaper short lengths of 2×4 construction-heart-grade redwood can serve as stringers. A rented power hammer makes fastening stringers to slab a simple matter of shooting rustproof concrete nails through both.

The second step of slab transformation is equally direct: fastening the decking to the stringers. Again, cheaper random lengths of 2×6 construction-common-grade redwood can be used—even for diagonal decking. For stability, each butt joint should meet over a stringer, and no two adjacent joints should be fastened to the same stringer (see photo). There should also be at least ⅛-inch drainage space between deck boards.

Once decking is nailed in place, the edges can be trimmed flush with the slab. In the deck shown here, the upper level was finished by power-hammering a 2×8 faceplate to the exposed concrete step.

The lower deck could be finished the same way. But here the designers chose to add a two-foot border that enhances deck appearance—and adds space. Framing for the border was con-

DECK OVER CONCRETE SLAB

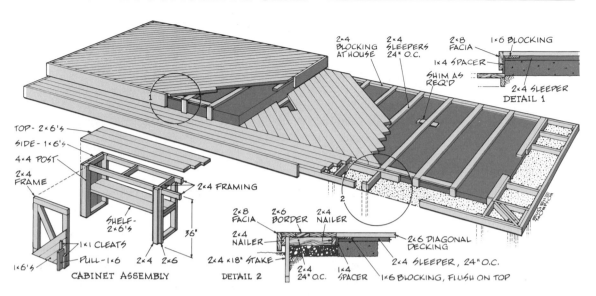

2×4 BLOCKING AT HOUSE

2×4 SLEEPERS 24" O.C.

2×8 FACIA

1×6 BLOCKING

1×4 SPACER

SHIM AS REQ'D

2×4 SLEEPER

DETAIL 1

TOP- 2×6'S

SIDE- 1×6'S

4×4 POST

2×4 FRAME

2×4 FRAMING

SHELF- 2×6'S

36"

1×1 CLEATS

PULL- 1×6

2×4   2×6

1×6'S

CABINET ASSEMBLY

2×8 FACIA

2×6 BORDER

2×4 NAILER

2×4 NAILER

2×4 ×18" STAKE

2×4 24" O.C.

1×4 SPACER

DETAIL 2

2×6 DIAGONAL DECKING

2×4 SLEEPER, 24" O.C.

1×6 BLOCKING, FLUSH ON TOP

To support diagonal decking, stringers should be laid 16 in. on center (diagram at top). For best drainage, they should be laid perpendicular to the house wall. Where the concrete slab is pitted or uneven, shims or small blocks should be used to level stringers before they're nailed to concrete. Storage cabinets (above) are built entirely of lumber—no plywood or other paneling is used. This makes for an exceptionally sturdy unit—one that can easily handle heavy garden supplies. For added design interest, the 1 × 6 handles stretch full height of door.

structed separately, using 2×4s braced every 2 feet. The frame sits on a bed of gravel in a shallow (two feet wide by one foot deep) trench. Concrete nails fasten its inner edge to the slab; the outer edge is nailed to 18-inch-high 2×4 stakes driven into the ditch at 2-foot intervals. A 2×8 facing and 2×6 decking complete the border.

For further construction data, send a stamped, self-addressed envelope to California Redwood Assn., 405 Enfrente Dr., Suite 200, Novato, CA 94949. Ask for *Construction Tips: Redwood Deck over Concrete.—Text by Susan Renner-Smith, drawings by Eugene Thompson.*

TUCK A TRELLIS DECK ALONG A WING

Often the key to staying put—bringing your current home in line with family needs instead of resorting to the disruption of moving to a larger house—is an addition of a room or two. But before you start to tear out a wall for a tack-on, give serious thought to what such a project can contribute toward your total living space.

These dramatic before-and-after photos show how Puget Sound homeowners transformed an ordinary house. They needed a home office/master bedroom suite so that existing

Before and after photos show the dramatic transformation of this Puget Sound home. New deck and room addition provide added living space for this growing family.

Dramatic conversion of a dreary slab into this inviting deck was achieved with sap-streaked redwood for decking, bench, planters, and built-in storage units. Diagonally laid decking and matching cabinet doors highlight design interest of yellow sapwood stripes.

91

Two back doors—each with its own concrete pad—dictated that any added deck be kept low. Author first staked out a rectangular area (right) then framed it cleverly (see pages 94–95) so outer corners could be given a special treatment (above).

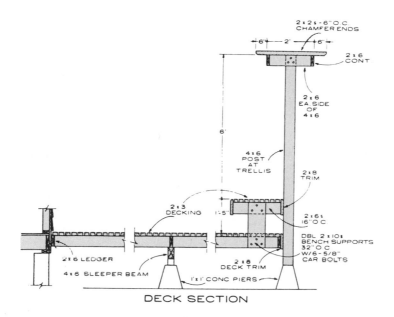

DECK SECTION

bedrooms could be freed for growing children. But the wing extension provided a bonus by creating a deep L, offering an outdoor space sheltered from neighbors and prevailing winds. The unappealing concrete slab at the back door was no longer adequate for this sumptuous new space, so the homeowners covered it with a patio deck, extending it 20 feet along the new wall. By planning this deck as an integral part of the addition, they simplified construction. Ledger boards to support deck joists were tied into the new framing.

To take advantage of the attractive view of the deck as well as the sunlight, they designed a glazed corner into the bedroom, with a separate sliding-glass-door access to the deck. Parents can relax indoors while keeping an eye on their youngest at play on the deck. And the entire area, with its built-in seating, is an ideal party space—something the small rooms and cramped patio of the original house never offered.

To lay the deck, the existing concrete slab was thoroughly cleaned and pressure-treated "sleepers"—staggered 2 × 4s laid face down— were anchored in beads of waterproof adhesive, in a pattern that allowed drainage runoff. Then redwood planks were nailed across these sleepers. But the planking extends well beyond the old slab. There it's nailed to joists conventionally supported on concrete piers. All the visible lumber for decking, perimeter benches and the trellis for hanging plants that backs one run of the bench (see section) is Construction Common and Construction Heart grade California redwood.

For a videotape on this entire project, send a check for $9.95 plus $2.95 for shipping (U.S. currency only) to InstructoVision, 9800 Bayard Ave. N.W., Seattle, WA 98117; ask for "Add-A-Room."—*Text by Alfred Lees, photos by Bob Strode.*

FLOAT A GROUND-LEVEL DECK OVER PADS

See color photo on page 92.

Like many homeowners, I have a back door—two in fact—set just inches above ground level. I wanted to hide the existing concrete pads by each door under a deck, but a conventional add-on would rise above my low thresholds, so I might have settled for an ugly slab patio instead.

Start construction by laying out stakes for footings for the rectangular deck. Position the beams on the footers so there's room to gang-nail joists from the angled corners. Drill before nailing the headers to the posts in angled corners to prevent splitting. Four pre-drilled posts secured to the joists with carriage bolts support the inner bench. The bench top rests on oversize cleats cut from 2 × 6s. Install posts for the seat-rail every 5 feet. To support 2 × 6 planks, attach 2 × 4s to the sides of each post, flush with the top. Insert blocking between the rails for more nailing surfaces.

FLOATING GROUND-LEVEL DECK

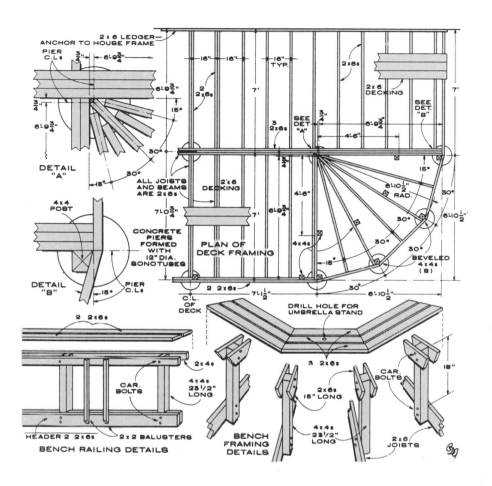

The solution: Raise a 14-by-28-foot deck just a fraction of an inch above grade on concrete footings, and float it over the pads. The beam and joist design would keep the deck low enough to fit under the doors. To dress up the deck and create maximum seating, I rounded off both outside corners. The built-in bench rail is topped with double 2×6 planks for a broad seat. Another built-in bench doubles as a table. You can adapt my design to float over any size patio slab by adjusting the placement of the footer piers.

Start construction by sinking the footers—except the four that will support the angled corners—below the frost line. Remember to extend the footers only a hair's breadth above grade, just enough to lift the pressure-treated lumber off the ground. You can position the four remaining footers, two on each side, after you've framed the rest of the deck.

Next, attach a ledger to the house. Then set the inside beam (I used triple 2×6 beams for my 28-foot run) in place on the footers. I didn't tie together the beams and footers; the ledger and the deck's weight will hold the structure in place. (If you live in an area that's often hit by gale-force winds, secure the beams to the footers with anchor plates.) Nail on joist hangers to attach joists to the ledger and beam. Lay the two remaining beams in place, and spike the three together.

Install the double 2×6 band joists, or headers, at the deck's front. Again, use hangers to secure joists to the header and beam. With the deck partially framed, you're ready to install the angled corners.

First, set the locations for the piers 30 and 60 degrees from the center beam (see drawing). Now, cut the beveled-end band joists to butt over these piers, as shown, and nail the 2×6 members together with the beveled 4×4 posts backing up the joints. Beveling is best done on a 10-inch radial-arm saw. If you haven't got one, you can either ask your local lumberyard to do the angle cutting or plane the bevels by hand.

To fit the posts into the beam-header or joist-header joints, set your saw for a 15-degree cut, then rip the post's face. For the header-to-header intersections, you need to double-bevel one face. Keep the saw set at 15 degrees, and rip to a center line down the post's face. Then turn the board end-for-end, and bevel the other half.

Next, install the joists that fan out from the center beam. Where they meet the band joist at a 90-degree angle, use joist hangers. When the angle was less than 90 degrees, I simply nailed the joist's outer end to the side of the post. This leaves these two joists offset, but won't show when the decking is applied. Then gang-nail the inner ends of these joists over the inside pier—there's no need to bevel them for a snugger fit.

Now you're ready to install the decking. I installed the planks at a 45-degree angle in the corners to create a pattern. To prevent the ends of the boards from lifting, I doubled up on the three center joists so that both sides of every butt joint were fully supported.—*Text by Mike McNally, photos by Coachman Studios and Greg Sharko.*

13 Second-Level Deck for Lofty Outdoor Living

O n warm summer days, it's hard to beat the ease and convenience of a deck, especially if it's located off the main living area of your house. Unfortunately, not every house has such a convenience—or if it does, it's often small and inadequate.

The deck shown on these pages graces the second-level dining and bedroom areas at the rear of a two-story tract home. Access is through sliding glass doors from the kitchen, and a window nearby serves as a pass-through for food and beverages served on the patio.

The deck is made entirely of construction heart redwood as classified by the California Redwood Assn. This lumber is natu-

Easy-to-climb stairs, wide railing, and attractive plant hangers are among features of handsome, functional elevated deck.

SECOND LEVEL DECK

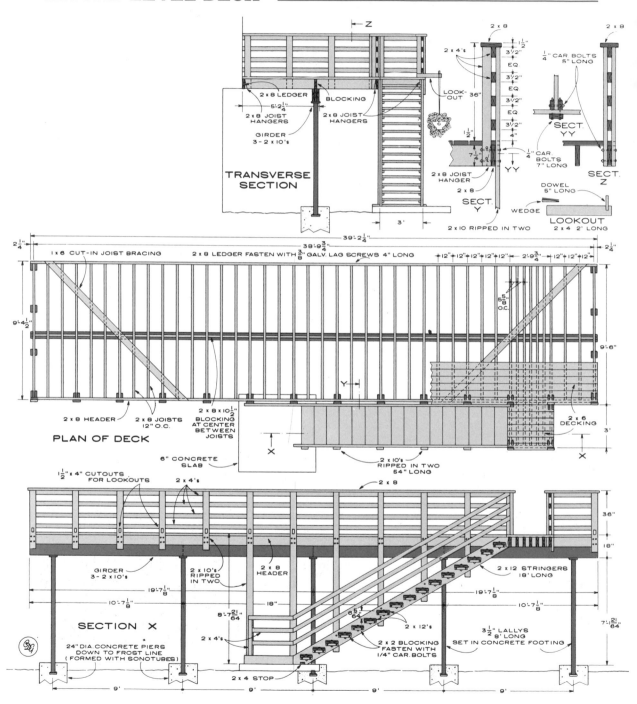

TRANSVERSE SECTION

2 x 8 LEDGER
5'-2¼"
2 x 8 JOIST HANGERS
BLOCKING
2 x 8 JOIST HANGERS
GIRDER 3 - 2 x 10's

LOOK-OUT
2 x 4's
2 x 8
36"
1½"
3½"
EQ
3½"
EQ
3½"
EQ
3½"
4"
7¼"
2 x 8 JOIST HANGER
2 x 8
2 x 10 RIPPED IN TWO

¼" CAR. BOLTS 5" LONG
SECT. YY
¼" CAR. BOLTS 7" LONG
SECT. Y
2 x 8
SECT. Z

DOWEL 5" LONG
WEDGE
LOOKOUT
2 x 4 2' LONG

PLAN OF DECK

39'-2¼"
38'-9¾"
2¼"
2¼"
1 x 6 CUT-IN JOIST BRACING
2 x 8 LEDGER FASTEN WITH ⅜" GALV. LAG SCREWS 4" LONG
12" 12" 12" 12" 12" 2'-9¾" 12" 12" 12"
5⅝" O.C.
9'-4½"
9'-6"
2 x 8 HEADER
2 x 8 JOISTS 12" O.C.
2 x 8 x 10½" BLOCKING AT CENTER BETWEEN JOISTS
6" CONCRETE SLAB
2 x 10's RIPPED IN TWO 54" LONG
2 x 6 DECKING
3'

SECTION X

1½" x 4" CUTOUTS FOR LOOKOUTS
2 x 4's
2 x 8
36"
18"
GIRDER 3 - 2 x 10's
2 x 10's RIPPED IN TWO
2 x 8 HEADER
19'-7⅛"
10'-7⅛"
8'-7²¹⁄₆₄"
2 x 4's
2 x 4 STOP
2 x 12's
2 x 2 BLOCKING FASTEN WITH ¼" CAR. BOLTS
6⅝¹⁄₆₄"
2 x 12 STRINGERS 18' LONG
19'-7⅛"
10'-7⅛"
3½" LALLYS 8' LONG SET IN CONCRETE FOOTING
7'-²¹⁄₆₄"
24" DIA. CONCRETE PIERS DOWN TO FROST LINE (FORMED WITH SONOTUBES)
9'
9'
9'
9'

98

How many beams to a cantilever?

Ideally, a deck attached to a house should be designed for a live load of 40 lbs. per square foot. The redwood deck shown here weighs 10 lbs. per square foot (its dead load). So the supports—the girder, Lally columns, and footings—had to be designed for a total deck load of 50 lbs. per square foot (40 lbs of live load plus 10 lbs. of dead load).

What about the cantilever, especially the long cantilever of the stair platform? When you calculate the load a cantilevered wood beam can bear, you figure it either with the load concentrated at the end of the cantilever or with the load evenly distributed along the length of the beam beyond the point of support. The distance from the girder to the ends of the joists on the stair platform is 7 feet. To find the uniformly distributed load that can be supported by one joist, use the formula:

$$W = \frac{fbd^2}{36L}$$

in which W = safe load (lbs.) uniformly distributed on joist; f = fiber stress (psi); b = width of joist (inches); d² = square of the depth of joist; and L = length of span (feet).

Fiber stress is a figure derived from laboratory tests. If you carefully select construction heart redwood with a close grain structure (eight rings or more per inch) and no splits, knots, or interrupted grain, its fiber stress will be about 1,000. Based on the formula, then:

$$W = \frac{1,000 \times 1.5 \times 7.25^2}{36 \times 7} = 312.87$$

One joist can safely support roughly 313 lbs.

The uniform loading of the long cantilever is 1,307 lbs. (found by multiplying the area of the cantilevered section by the total load of 50 lbs. per square foot). Add to that one-half the load of the upper half of the stairs, or 800 lbs. (calculated by multiplying an average 200-lb. load for each tread times eight treads and dividing by half). The total load, then, that must be supported by the 7-foot cantilever is 2,108 lbs.

To determine the number of joists necessary to support the total weight, divide the total load by the capacity of each joist:

$$\frac{2,108}{313} = 6.74$$

Seven joists are needed, spaced to fit as shown, but they must be held together in such a manner that they support the entire distributed load as a unit. The girder itself is a built-up beam constructed from redwood 2 × 10s pieced together as shown below.

20'			20'	
11'		18'		11'
20'			20'	

MATERIALS LIST FOR DECK

All lumber is construction-grade heart redwood.

Stringers and treads: five 2 × 12s, each 20 feet long; three 2 × 12s, each 16 feet long

Girder: five 2 × 10s, each 20 feet long; two 2 × 10s, each 12 feet long

Short joists, ledger, deck header, shelf, and railing: 28 2 × 8s, each 20 feet long

Long joists: seven 2 × 8s, each 14 feet long

Stringer supports and post fasciae: four 2 × 10s, each 20 feet long

Posts and rails: 23 2 × 4s, each 20 feet long; six 2 × 4s, each 18 feet long

Decking: 42 2 × 6s, each 20 feet long

Deck bracing: two 1 × 6s, each 20 feet long

rally resistant to insects and decay and—like all redwood—is dimensionally stable and easy to work with using ordinary tools. You'll need a portable power drill and circular saw.

The deck is supported by five Lally columns, each 8 feet long. The columns are set 1-foot-deep in concrete piers, which in turn extend to below the frost line.

The deck is 40 feet long and 9½ feet wide. It has exceptionally clean lines, with the front plank of decking set between railing posts so no butt joints are exposed, and with all bolt heads located to be an element of the design.

Building the deck is a straightforward job. After installing the Lally columns, allow the concrete to cure thoroughly, then fasten the main girder to the top plates. Use ¼-by-3-inch galvanized lag screws.

Fasten the 2 × 8 ledger board to the header at the house's second level so that its lower edge is ½-inch higher than the top of the girder—this gives a slight slope to the deck for better drainage. Use ⅜-inch galvanized lag screws 4 inches long on 1-foot centers.

Support joists for stair-landing platform run seven feet past the main girder. To support the load, the joists must be narrowly spaced, properly blocked, and secured with steel hangers as shown so that the total load is transferred to and supported by *all* of the joists. Nail the hangers to the joists at the platform blocking and ends before attaching them to the house ledger: There's very little room to swing a hammer with this spacing.

Fasten the joists to the ledger with 2 × 8 joist hangers. The main deck joists are cut to 9 feet 1½ inches from 10-foot lengths. The waste is used for the blocking between joists (located at the center of the girder). Fasten the joist blocking with 10d hot-dip-galvanized nails.

After placing the 2 × 8 deck header and the 2 × 4 railing posts, cut into the tops of joists for the 1 × 6 bracing shown on the plan and fasten securely. Now the 2 × 6 decking can be laid, again using 10d galvanized nails.

Assemble the railing and stair supports as shown in the drawings. Note that the 2 × 8 railing is mitered at all corners. Where it's butted along straight lengths, it's joined with 45-degree diagonals.

The stringers and treads of the stairs are cut from 2 × 12s. Treads are 11¼ inches wide with a rise of 6⁵⁄₆₄ inches. This combination makes the stairway easy to climb up and down—there's no need to negotiate high steps. Support the treads on 2 × 2 cleats attached with carriage bolts.

The stair stringer located closest to the deck is supported by 2 × 10s ripped in two, which are attached with ¼-inch carriage bolts. Both stringers are attached to the upper platform with 2 × 8 joist hangers. Secure the stringers to the concrete base with a 2 × 4 stringer stop that's anchored to the concrete.

The plant hangers are made from 2 × 4s drilled for a 1-inch-diameter dowel; they are wedged into the cutouts drilled and chiseled through the railing posts.

The natural finish of the redwood can be maintained with clear water repellent and mildewcide applied immediately after completion and every two years thereafter. This tends to mellow the color to a shade of buckskin tan. If left unfinished, or if the water-repellent treatment is discontinued, the deck will gradually weather to a driftwood gray. If you want a permanent redwood color (or some other color tone), use a lightly pigmented deck stain or bleach.—*Text and drawings by Carl DeGroote, photos by Greg Sharko.*

14 High-Rise Planter Deck

Rising above rolling New Jersey woodland is a garden on a redwood deck. The high garden provides a protected planting area for herbs, vegetables, and annual flowers—a welcome respite from marauding groundhogs, deer, and rabbits. I designed the deck as an architectonic complement to a colonial-style tract house. The bold angled railing, formed by the 3-foot-high planters, creates two "rooms" for alfresco dining and sunbathing. Each room has a "window" defined by a section of open railing. The deck, 9 feet above the sloping site, is reached by a redwood stairway from the driveway and by a door from the utility room.

I use the colonnaded covered space under the deck to protect summering house plants and for a shady seating area; 8-inch-diameter Wolmanized utility poles create the shady loggia. The poles rest on pins sunk into 2×2-foot concrete footings that extend below the frost line. Double beams bolted together are notched into the poles to form a continuous column capital. All bolts and nails are hot-dipped galvanized. Wood blocking bolted at the midpoint of the spans provides structural integrity. I specified shallow 2×8 redwood beams and joists to keep the underside of the deck as high as possible. The poles continue through the beams to support another set of double 2×8 beams, which support the redwood planters. The 16-inch-on-center 2×8 joists rest in joist hangers nailed to a ledger plate bolted to the house. The 2×4 redwood decking is laid diagonally across the joists at a 45-degree angle. Rather than attaching the decking with the usual flathead galvanized nails, I used 10-penny button-head nails suggested by the builder, Allan Sheppard of North Plainfield, N.J. These give a unique, finished look.

The planters, framed and sheathed in redwood, are lined

102

Nine-foot-high columns support planter deck and provide a shady loggia underneath (right). Deck has two activity areas: one for dining, another for sunbathing (above).

HIGH-RISE PLANTER DECK

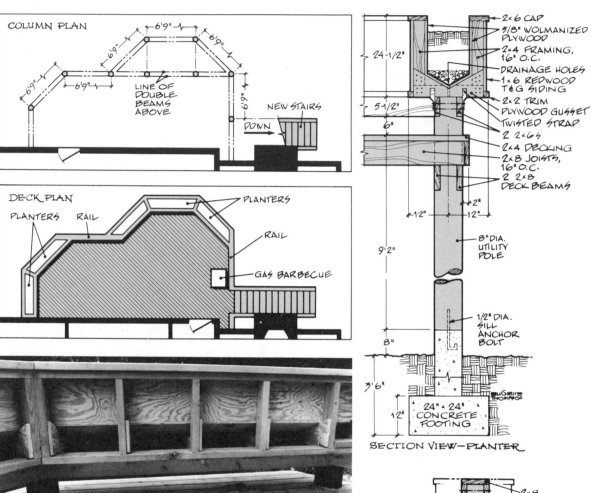

COLUMN PLAN

6'9" 6'9" 6'9"

6'9"

6'9"

LINE OF
DOUBLE
BEAMS
ABOVE

NEW STAIRS

DOWN

DECK PLAN

PLANTERS

PLANTERS RAIL

RAIL

GAS BARBECUE

2×6 CAP
5/8" WOLMANIZED
PLYWOOD
2×4 FRAMING,
16" O.C.
DRAINAGE HOLES
1×6 REDWOOD
T&G SIDING
2×2 TRIM
PLYWOOD GUSSET
TWISTED STRAP
2 2×6s
2×4 DECKING
2×8 JOISTS,
16" O.C.
2 2×8
DECK BEAMS

24-1/2"

5 1/2"

6"

9'2"

8"

3'6"

2"

12" 12"

8"DIA.
UTILITY
POLE

1/2" DIA.
SILL
ANCHOR
BOLT

12" 24"×24"
CONCRETE
FOOTING

SECTION VIEW—PLANTER

Planters were built in modules. After precutting components,
builder set up a jig and nailed together frame sections, bracing
with plywood. These were toenailed on 16 inches center to 2 × 8
beams. Frames were sheathed inside with ½-inch Wolmanized
plywood, on the outside with 1 × 6 redwood siding.

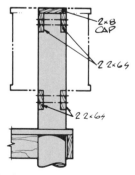

2×8
CAP

2 2×6s

2 2×6s

SECTION VIEW—RAIL

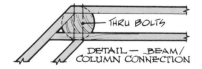

THRU BOLTS

DETAIL—BEAM/
COLUMN CONNECTION

BLOCKING THRU BOLT

DETAIL—BEAMS AT MID-SPAN

Tops of columns were cut off level to support planters (above left). Columns rest on concrete footings, which extend below frost line (above, right). The 2 × 8 redwood ledger plate, bolted to the house, has joist hangers nailed to it, which support 2 × 8 redwood joists (right).

with Wolmanized plywood. I coated the inside face of the plywood with Karnak Asphaltic DL emulsion No. 330 to protect it from constant moisture. Half-inch holes drilled into the bottom of each planter section permit drainage.—*Text and design by Amy Delson, A.I.A.; photos by Greg Sharko; drawings by Eugene Thompson.*

15 Deck with Butcher-Block Built-ins

If a deck turns out to be just a place to sit or lounge, why bother? I could just as well set a chair out on the grass. That thought ran through my mind as I planned the deck for my backyard. Mine had to offer some useful amenities.

The result is a comfortable lounging area with character. The deck has a triangular table that is easier to get to than most picnic tables. The benches are roomy enough for sunbathers to lie with their arms along their sides.

The deck is open—my backyard isn't obscured by seat backs or railings. The support beams are recessed, giving the effect of reduced mass, and overhead rafters shade outdoor lighting fixtures and support hanging plants.

Construction was straightforward, as you can see from the

See color photo on page 109.

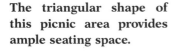

The triangular shape of this picnic area provides ample seating space.

BUTCHER BLOCK BUILT-INS

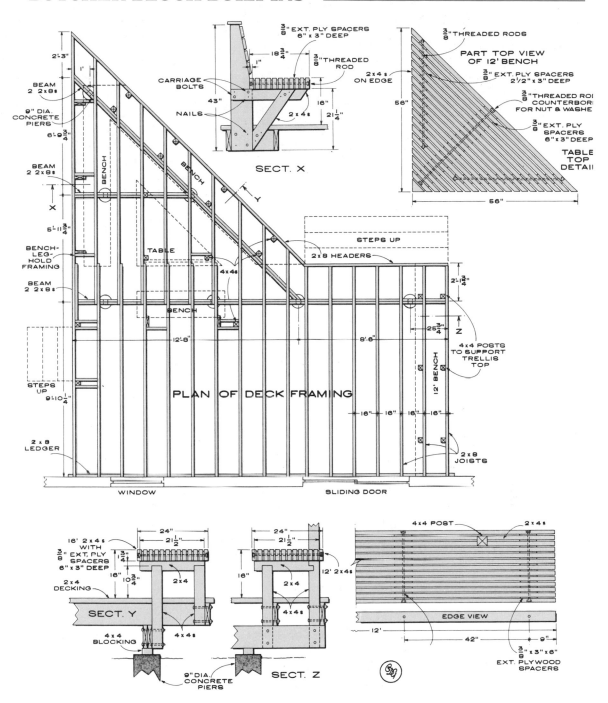

$\frac{3}{8}$" EXT. PLY SPACERS 6" x 3" DEEP

18$\frac{3}{4}$"

$\frac{3}{8}$" THREADED ROD

1"

CARRIAGE BOLTS

43"

NAILS

16"

21$\frac{1}{4}$"

2 x 4 s

SECT. X

$\frac{3}{8}$" THREADED RODS

PART TOP VIEW OF 12' BENCH

$\frac{3}{8}$" EXT. PLY SPACERS 2$\frac{1}{2}$" x 3" DEEP

2 x 4 s ON EDGE

56"

$\frac{3}{8}$" THREADED ROD COUNTERBORE FOR NUT & WASHER

$\frac{3}{8}$" EXT. PLY SPACERS 6" x 3" DEEP

TABLE TOP DETAIL

56"

2'-3"

1"

BEAM 2 2 x 8 s

9" DIA. CONCRETE PIERS

6'-9$\frac{3}{4}$"

BEAM 2 2 x 8 s

X

5'-11$\frac{3}{4}$"

BEAM 2 2 x 8 s

BENCH LEG HOLD FRAMING

BEAM 2 2 x 8 s

STEPS UP

9'-10$\frac{1}{4}$"

2 x 8 LEDGER

BENCH

BENCH

Y

TABLE

4 x 4 s

BENCH

12'-8"

PLAN OF DECK FRAMING

STEPS UP

2 x 8 HEADERS

2'-1$\frac{3}{4}$"

Z

2 5$\frac{3}{4}$"

8'-6"

12' BENCH

16" 16" 16" 16"

4 x 4 POSTS TO SUPPORT TRELLIS TOP

2 x 8 JOISTS

WINDOW

SLIDING DOOR

4 x 4 POST

2 x 4 s

16' 2 x 4 s WITH $\frac{3}{8}$" EXT. PLY SPACERS 6" x 3" DEEP

24"

21$\frac{1}{2}$"

$\frac{3}{4}$"

16"

10$\frac{3}{4}$"

2 x 4

2 x 4 DECKING

SECT. Y

4 x 4 BLOCKING

4 x 4 s

9" DIA. CONCRETE PIERS

24"

21$\frac{1}{2}$"

16"

2 x 4

12' 2 x 4 s

4 x 4 s

SECT. Z

EDGE VIEW

12'

42"

9"

$\frac{3}{8}$" x 3" x 6" EXT. PLYWOOD SPACERS

107

The ledger with joist hangers is in place. Black polyethylene sheet was laid to prevent growth of weeds under deck. Joists must be level. Penetrating preservative applied to all the trimmed surfaces helps prevent wood deterioration (right).

plans. Some areas needed special attention, however. To build the benches, particular accuracy was needed both in measuring the dimensions for the lumber and in positioning each hole (for threaded rods) drilled in the 2×4s used on the seating platforms. Use pressure-treated lumber throughout.

I cut the lumber prior to assembly, with the exception of the top of the long diagonal bench, which I trimmed after I put it together.

To make the triangular table I first drew the table pattern on a large piece of paper (it could have been traced with chalk on a flat concrete surface). Next I laid out precut 2×4s and ⅜-inch plywood spacers on the pattern to be sure each piece was the right length. I then drew a center line from the triangle's apex to the base. Using this line as a guide I drilled ⁷⁄₁₆-inch holes through the sides of each 2×4 (with the exception of the piece at the apex). I drilled the exposed surface of the base piece 1½ inches deep so that all of the connecting-rod ends (and nuts) would be recessed.

I then secured all the 2×4s and spacers with a threaded rod by first placing the spacers between the 2×4s (including the spacers at both sides of the triangle), then inserting the threaded rod through the center-line holes and tightening the nuts on the rod.

Steps lead to the yard from the handsome deck at the rear of this modest home (right). The lounge area provides a place to sunbathe or gather for wining and dining. The decorative rafters serve as hanging racks for outdoor plants.

A favorite shade tree in this backyard was no obstacle to adding a spacious deck to this suburban Ohio home. In fact, it became a featured element in the design. (See Chapter 16)

Measuring 3 inches in from each side of the triangle, I drew a line parallel to the table's edge on each side. The lines stopped at the sixth 2×4 from the apex. I disassembled the table and drilled ⅝-inch holes (at a 45-degree angle at the points where the lines indicated) through the side of each 2×4 and spacer, aligned all the pieces, inserted the threaded rods, and tightened all the connections. Then I attached the table's apex piece and spacer with countersunk wood screws.

When laying the decking I started from the steps and worked toward the house, then out to the point of the triangular area of the deck. This helped ensure that even the last board was parallel to the house.

The completed deck has become one of the most active parts of my home—just as I'd hoped it would.—*Text and photos by Joseph W. Robicheau.*

16 Pedestal Deck Can Wrap Around a Tree

I magine dining out under leafy limbs or spending an afternoon with a good book under a favorite source of shade. What you've imagined can easily be yours. This attractive deck can wrap around a tree (or trees) to create a fresh setting for family barbecues and outdoor relaxation.

The contemporary diagonal lines of this elegant deck belie how easy it is to build. The deck is supported by 17 4 × 4 posts spaced about 6 feet apart; be sure that the wood is preservative-treated for ground-contact use. Drill two holes at right angles through the base of each post to take 10-inch lengths of steel reinforcing bars, which will anchor the posts. After digging 36-inch-deep holes at each post location and putting about two inches of gravel in the bottom of each for drainage, brace the posts upright, and pour in 14 to 16 inches of concrete.

The beams are 2 × 8s bolted to opposite sides of the posts with 3/8-by-8-inch hot-dipped galvanized carriage bolts, with a 1-inch washer and a lock washer preceding the nut. I used 3/8-by-6-inch lag bolts to tie beam pieces together wherever they intersected. All hardware should be plated, galvanized, or cement coated. The beams should provide a slope of about 1/16-inch per foot to drain rainwater or melting snow away from the house.

Once you have the beams in place, I recommend laying 2 inches of bank-run gravel under the deck. This surface eliminates puddles, which are nesting places for mosquitoes, but won't impede water flow to tree roots. It also discourages weed growth.

The joists were laid on 24-inch centers, using twisted steel straps called hurricane anchors. This device limits the number of times you have to toenail each joist to its beam, which should

See color photo on page 110.

This deck's low, open railing allows an optimum view of the yard.

make construction much easier. Nail the strap to the beam with 2-inch roofing nails. The strap has a right-angle twist and lines up with the joist; finish the job with roofing nails. Toenailing with 16d nails is needed only when a joist crosses a beam at other than a right angle.

With the joists in place, frame a box around the tree. You may also want to put up a joist extension for stairway or skirt support. Bolt the 2 × 4 vertical uprights for rail supports to the joists.

My plan shows these rail supports at the edge of the deck, but if you set them back a foot or more, you'll emphasize the deck's cantilever. With a low railing such a projection also provides a safety factor. A perimeter joist skirt further accents the canti-levered look.

Use 16d nails to secure the 2 × 4 deck boards. There should be ⅛- to ¼-inch between boards to allow water runoff. One simple way to ensure uniform spacing is to use a jig. I cut several U-shaped pieces from ¼-inch wood scrap and hung them over each joist. But even the best grades of lumber are subject to

113

PEDESTAL DECK

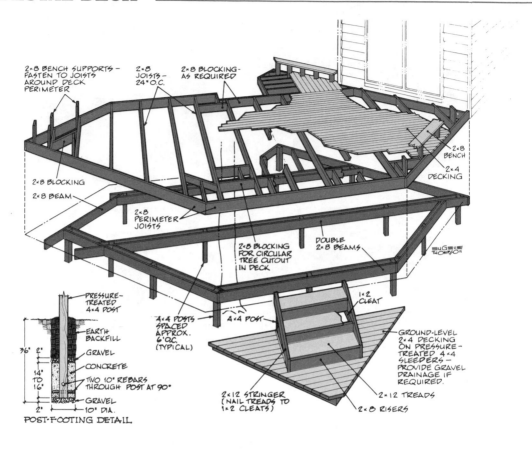

2×8 BENCH SUPPORTS—FASTEN TO JOISTS AROUND DECK PERIMETER

2×8 JOISTS—24" O.C.

2×8 BLOCKING—AS REQUIRED

2×8 BENCH

2×4 DECKING

2×8 BLOCKING

2×8 BEAM

2×8 PERIMETER JOISTS

2×8 BLOCKING FOR CIRCULAR TREE CUTOUT IN DECK

DOUBLE 2×8 BEAMS

PRESSURE-TREATED 4×4 POST

EARTH BACKFILL

GRAVEL

CONCRETE

TWO 10" REBARS THROUGH POST AT 90°

GRAVEL

10" DIA.

36"

2"

14" TO 16"

2"

POST-FOOTING DETAIL

4×4 POSTS SPACED APPROX. 6'O.C. (TYPICAL)

4×4 POST

1×2 CLEAT

GROUND-LEVEL 2×4 DECKING ON PRESSURE-TREATED 4×4 SLEEPERS—PROVIDE GRAVEL DRAINAGE IF REQUIRED.

2×12 STRINGER (NAIL TREADS TO 1×2 CLEATS)

2×8 RISERS

2×12 TREADS

No ledger need be bolted to the house wall when the deck is freestanding. Support posts are sunk below the frost line, and deck beams are bolted to both sides.

114

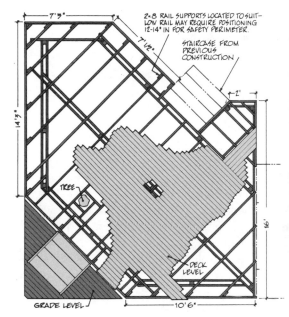

2×8 RAIL SUPPORTS LOCATED TO SUIT-LOW RAIL MAY REQUIRE POSITIONING 12-14" IN FOR SAFETY PERIMETER.

STAIRCASE FROM PREVIOUS CONSTRUCTION

7'3"

7'½"

14'3"

TREE

16'

DECK LEVEL

GRADE LEVEL

10'6"

1'

Once the joist network is in place, posts can be trimmed flush with the top of the grid, and the framing around the tree can be installed.

mild warpage, which can throw off the spacing. If you discover, as you proceed, that the boards aren't equally spaced, adjust gradually.

Snap a chalk line across the board ends when they are all in place, and cut along this with a portable circular saw. For a neater effect I then used my router to cut a quarter-round edge around the trimmed end of each plank. Cut the railings to height and install the railing cap. For my second stairway I used wooden steps I'd moved away from the kitchen door, snugging them into a niche in the joist skirt.

This deck offers a bonus that you may not have considered: storage space. Below your deck is room for oversize objects, such as a ladder, that take up too much room elsewhere.

The open area around the deck can be dressed up with pre-fabricated, treated diagonal lattice panels. These panels, available in either 2-by-4- or 4-by-8-foot sections, carry the diagonals of the deck right down to ground level and will save your storage from being an eyesore.—*Text and photos by James R. Heaton, drawings by Eugene Thompson.*

17 Latticed Backyard Retreat

What could be better than drinking cool lemonade and relaxing in an airy backyard gazebo that also offers a bit of privacy from close neighbors? Using low-maintenance redwood lumber and lattice panels (in 2-by-8- and 4-by-8-foot sizes), a homeowner with basic carpentry skills and tools can build this structure in a couple of weekends. You can decide whether to build the gazebo as a cozy corner retreat or as a central backyard focal point; my choice was the latter. The redwood lattice provides dappled shade (augmented by nearby trees) while letting cooling breezes waft through.

To build the gazebo, set the outer posts of the structure first, making sure they are plumb before setting the additional front deck-support posts in line with them. I set the posts 3 feet into the ground without using concrete.

Use zinc-plated carriage bolts for additional strength and rust resistance when attaching the 2×6 deck-support stringers to the support posts. Nail on the front 2×6 facing, which will support the front deck 2×4.

When I laid the 2×4 deck boards, I left a ⅜-inch space between boards for drainage. Wait until the deck is attached before trimming the 2×4s to match the structural angles. Give the top of the structure a front-to-back slope of about 7 inches (or 5 percent) to give an illusion of spaciousness.

When it's time to attach the upper front 2×6 facing, be sure the front posts are the same distance apart at the deck and at the top. Nail on 2×4s to complete the top framing after rabbeting their inner faces to take the overhead lattice sections. Vertical lattice sections can be attached to the upright framing in one of two ways, depending on the tools you have. Either cut a groove in 2×2s the width of the lattice, as shown, or nail beveled cleats on each side of the lattice. One edge of each vertical

Redwood lattice panels add a breezy charm to this decorative gazebo deck that gets you comfortably off the damp lawn.

2 × 2 or cleat will need to be cut at an angle its full length to match the angle it will set against the 4 × 4 post.

The lattice sections can be easily cut with either a handsaw or power saw, but handle the panels carefully to avoid dislodging the staples used in their construction. I designed the two front side sections at a shorter 45-inch height to give the structure a more open, airy feeling. The back panel is in two sections, with the top one hinged so you have the option of closing it for additional screening or dropping it for more ventilation. To wind up construction, you can add triangular decorative trim at the upper front corners.

When the structure is completed, apply a preservative like Woodlife. Afterward, you can apply a redwood stain if you wish to retain the red color. If no stain is applied, all redwood gradually changes to a weathered gray color.

Your own personal touches complete your leisure retreat. Twin cushioned redwood chairs on the deck invite backyard relaxing, and a matching chaise lounge may attract sunbathers to the semiprivate area in front of the structure. The intriguing design of the redwood lattice invites creative use of the remaining scrap, such as forming a border trim along the front of an adjoining flower bed.—*Text and photos by Louis Poppe, drawings by Gerhard Richter.*

117

LATTICED BACKYARD RETREAT

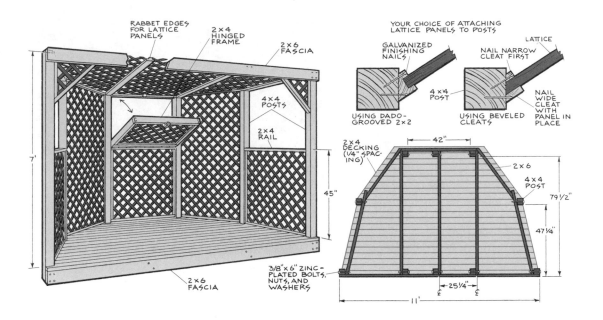

It's a good idea to cover the ground under the structure with a heavy-grade plastic ground cover held down by gravel or rubble (right) to prevent the growth of weeds.

18 Hinged Deck Sections Shutter Glass

My first experience with a problem-solving deck was when I designed one for my own leisure home. I'd proposed to *Popular Science* that my major project contribution to the magazine's special Centennial issue be an innovative build-it-yourself house for the type of rugged site that's likely to be found on the remote mountainside or waterfront properties that are still available in this crowded world. Because a weekend or vacation home will almost certainly be blessed with a view, I wanted this house to have a front wall of glass.

But that would make the home vulnerable to rough weather and vandalism while its owners were away. So, working with my architect, I devised and installed (with co-builder Ron Nelson) a deck that featured hinged sections that could be easily raised to shutter the glass wall each time I closed the house—for a weekend or a winter. I've now put this system to effective use for the 17 years I've enjoyed this house and can recommend the principle to anyone with a second home.

The security function comes as a bonus, without compromising the primary function of any deck—its recreational use. A deck is really an outdoor room added to any home, and in a compact house like mine, it's vital for entertaining. So I ran my support posts on up through the deck for a built-in perimeter bench that provides lots of seating.

My home is a pole house—that is, it hangs within massive support poles and requires no foundation (which makes it ideal for "unbuildable" sites that are too steep or rocky or sandy for excavations and conventional footings). Since the frame of my deck is tied into the beam that supports my glass wall, I've included a sketch of a typical pole foundation. The outer end of my deck is supported on 6 × 6 posts (in my case, made up by

When this house is closed for the winter, two hinged sections of the redwood-plank deck fold up against the glass doors and bolt in the raised position from inside the house. Exit is then made through a solid-panel door at the top of the upper stairs (above). A bonus of having the deck raised during winter is that snow won't pile up on open joists.

For a winter visit, the hinged sections are easily lowered (left). To protect the exposed upper edges of the raised sections, author added an awning (above) of plywood panels that the sections tuck beneath. This keeps the edges free of snow or rain. The triangular brackets are lag-screwed to a structural beam.

HINGED DECK

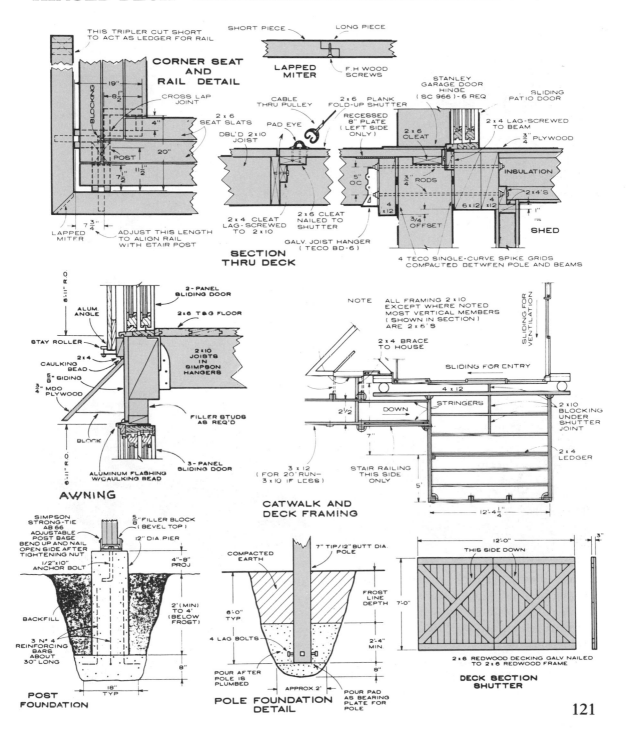

CORNER SEAT AND RAIL DETAIL

THIS TRIPLER CUT SHORT TO ACT AS LEDGER FOR RAIL

BLOCKING

19"
8½"

CROSS LAP JOINT

2×6 SEAT SLATS

4"

POST

20"

7½"   11½"

7¾"

LAPPED MITER

ADJUST THIS LENGTH TO ALIGN RAIL WITH STAIR POST

LAPPED MITER

SHORT PIECE   LONG PIECE

F.H WOOD SCREWS

SECTION THRU DECK

CABLE THRU PULLEY

PAD EYE

DBL'D 2×10 JOIST

2×4 CLEAT LAG-SCREWED TO 2×10

2×6 CLEAT NAILED TO SHUTTER

2×6 PLANK FOLD-UP SHUTTER

RECESSED 8" PLATE (LEFT SIDE ONLY)

GALV. JOIST HANGER (TECO BD-6)

STANLEY GARAGE DOOR HINGE (SC 966)-6 REQ

SLIDING PATIO DOOR

2×6 CLEAT

2×4 LAG-SCREWED TO BEAM

¾ PLYWOOD

INSULATION

2×4'S

5" OC

¾" RODS

4×12   6×12   4×12

1"

¾" OFFSET

SHED

4 TECO SINGLE-CURVE SPIKE GRIDS COMPACTED BETWEEN POLE AND BEAMS

AWNING

6'-11" RO

ALUM. ANGLE

STAY ROLLER

2×4

CAULKING BEAD

⅝" SIDING

4¾" MDO PLYWOOD

BLOCK

2-PANEL SLIDING DOOR

2×6 T&G FLOOR

2×10 JOISTS IN SIMPSON HANGERS

FILLER STUDS AS REQ'D

3-PANEL SLIDING DOOR

ALUMINUM FLASHING W/CAULKING BEAD

6'-11" RO

CATWALK AND DECK FRAMING

NOTE ALL FRAMING 2×10 EXCEPT WHERE NOTED MOST VERTICAL MEMBERS (SHOWN IN SECTION) ARE 2×6'S

2×4 BRACE TO HOUSE

SLIDING FOR ENTRY

SLIDING FOR VENTILATION

4×12

2½"

DOWN

STRINGERS

2×10 BLOCKING UNDER SHUTTER JOINT

2×4 LEDGER

7"

3×12 (FOR 20' RUN- 3×10 IF LESS)

STAIR RAILING THIS SIDE ONLY

5'

12'-4¼"

POST FOUNDATION

SIMPSON STRONG-TIE AB 66 ADJUSTABLE POST BASE BEND UP AND NAIL OPEN SIDE AFTER TIGHTENING NUT

½"×10" ANCHOR BOLT

BACKFILL

3 N° 4 REINFORCING BARS ABOUT 30" LONG

⅝" FILLER BLOCK (BEVEL TOP)

12" DIA PIER

4"-8" PROJ

2'(MIN) TO 4' (BELOW FROST)

8"

18" TYP

POLE FOUNDATION DETAIL

7" TIP/12" BUTT DIA. POLE

COMPACTED EARTH

6'-0" TYP

4 LAG BOLTS

POUR AFTER POLE IS PLUMBED

APPROX 2'

POUR PAD AS BEARING PLATE FOR POLE

FROST LINE DEPTH

2'-4" MIN

8"

DECK SECTION SHUTTER

12'-0"

THIS SIDE DOWN

3"

7'-0"

2×6 REDWOOD DECKING GALV. NAILED TO 2×6 REDWOOD FRAME

121

OTHER DECK DETAILS

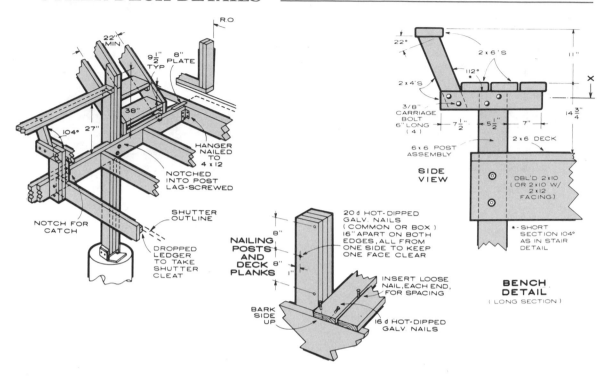

22" MIN

9½" TYP

8" PLATE

RO

38"

104° 27"

HANGER NAILED TO 4 x 12

NOTCHED INTO POST LAG-SCREWED

NOTCH FOR CATCH

SHUTTER OUTLINE

DROPPED LEDGER TO TAKE SHUTTER CLEAT

NAILING POSTS AND DECK PLANKS

8"

8"

1"

BARK SIDE UP

20 d HOT-DIPPED GALV. NAILS (COMMON OR BOX) 16" APART ON BOTH EDGES, ALL FROM ONE SIDE TO KEEP ONE FACE CLEAR

INSERT LOOSE NAIL, EACH END, FOR SPACING

16 d HOT-DIPPED GALV NAILS

22°

112°

2 x 6'S

2 x 4'S

3/8" CARRIAGE BOLT 6" LONG (4)

6 x 6 POST ASSEMBLY

SIDE VIEW

7½"

5½"

7"

11"

X

14¾"

2 x 6 DECK

DBL'D 2x10 (OR 2x10 W/ 2x12 FACING)

* - SHORT SECTION 104° AS IN STAIR DETAIL

BENCH DETAIL
(LONG SECTION)

Loose planks—gapped to match stationary section of deck—are assembled into panels by means of a half-lapped frame, here being glued in place with construction adhesive prior to being nailed with two 10-penny nails into each plank. (Note in plans sketch that one section has an extra plank, to cover this expanse of glass.) Clearance notches for this cross-buck underframe must be chiseled in the joists so that lowered deck sections will set flat on the support frame. To locate notches, lay assembled section in place on the deck frame and reach up from below to mark joists. Then cut two 1½-inch-deep saw kerfs, chisel out between (right).

122

Turning a corner with a built-in bench involves some tricky support framing. At left, author drills through sandwich of 2 × 4s to insert a carriage bolt. Finished bench stops short of open framing for hinged section (right), which will rest on the ledger when it's lowered.

face-nailing three 2 × 6s). These posts—unlike my embedded poles—are nailed into metal bases that are in turn anchored to concrete piers, as shown in the Post Foundation sketch.

I chose redwood for my deck, but it could be duplicated in pressure-treated lumber if you prefer. I gave each piece a flowing brush-coat of clear preservative as I readied it for assembly, a second coat when construction was complete. The workability of redwood is a delight, of course. It's pitch-free and compliant: planing, chiseling, drilling and nailing go faster than with other softwoods. Judicious predrilling assures you'll never split out, even close to edges and ends.

One disadvantage is that redwood mills rarely ship 6 × 6 posts. I turned the disadvantage of having to "layer" mine of 2 × 6s by trimming some of these triplers back to accept cross members, as shown in the sketches. This actually strengthens the whole structure. (Such assemblies don't quite fill the metal post bases, so I tucked a beveled scrap of my T 1-11 siding against one face before nailing the bases shut.)

Marine-supply outlets should be able to sell you inexpensive winches with an on-off ratchet and 3:1 gear, and perhaps 25-foot lengths of 3/16-inch-diameter steel cable with scissor hooks at one end. They should also stock chromed pad eyes that are the right size to accept these hooks. Don't skimp on attaching either the winches or the pad eyes (you'll need one of each for each section, of course): these assembled deck sections are heavy. Be sure to stand clear of them during raising and lowering procedures.—*Text by Alfred Lees; photos by the author, by Ron Nelson and Ed Wesch.*

123

19 Fast Decking with Drop-in Deck Squares

The step was added to the walkway by increasing the joist height. A cut and re-cleated square creates the angle above the step.

See color photos on page 127.

124

It's almost like laying tiles over an inside floor: Grab a panel, drop it in place, and move on to the next. However, Deck Squares are larger, so the job goes even faster.

Create a new patio with the squares, or use them to cover an existing slab that's cracked or pitted. "Install a new walkway," says Ken Woodfill, sales manager for Ajax YardWorks, maker of Deck Squares (3325 Ferguson Rd., Fort Wayne, Ind. 46809). "You can even make different sire planters or a border bench to dress up your deck."

If that sounds like there's a lot left to your imagination, you're right. That's one of the main advantages of Deck Squares.

The slatted squares come preassembled in two sizes—2 or 3 feet square—and are pressure-treated for a 20-year lifetime with no additional finishing. To cover an old slab, you merely lay the squares on top of the concrete surface. If there's an overlap at the slab edges, trim the Deck Squares to fit. To hold the squares in place, nail a finishing strip around the perimeter.

If you wish to extend the squares past the slab, add support joists as shown in the drawing below. Place 2 × 6s (for an average-height slab) around the slab's perimeter, and use these boards as the anchor points for the extension joists. The joists are placed in a 24- or 36-inch on-center grid pattern (depending on the size of the squares you choose); Deck Squares are placed on top and held with 2½-inch galvanized nails.

Similarly, a grid pattern of joists is used to create a new patio. (Ajax supplies a grid planning sheet.) Once the joists are installed, the first square is nailed in place at one corner. The edge of the square should cover only half the width of the next joist, allowing room to mount the adjacent square. All squares are

DECK-SQUARES DECK PLAN

If you are using the squares to cover a concrete slab and want to extend them, you can add support joists as shown in the diagram.

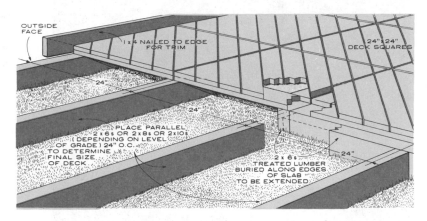

OUTSIDE FACE

1 x 4 NAILED TO EDGE FOR TRIM

24"x24" DECK SQUARES

24"

24"

PLACE PARALLEL 2 x 6s OR 2 x 8s OR 2 x 10s (DEPENDING ON LEVEL OF GRADE) 24" O.C. TO DETERMINE FINAL SIZE OF DECK

2 x 6 s TREATED LUMBER BURIED ALONG EDGES OF SLAB TO BE EXTENDED

24"

DECK-SQUARES DECK AND PLANTER

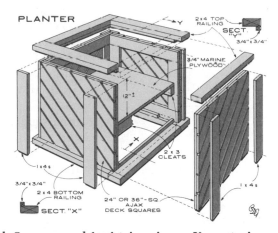

PLANTER

2 x 4 TOP RAILING

SECT. "Y"

3/4" x 3/4"

3/4" MARINE PLYWOOD

12"±

2 x 3 CLEATS

1 x 4 s

3/4" x 3/4"

2 x 4 BOTTOM RAILING

SECT. "X"

24" OR 36"-SQ AJAX DECK SQUARES

1 x 4 s

Flower planter is easily assembled using four Deck Squares and 1 × 4 trim pieces. Use exterior ply for the shelf; its height in the box depends on the size of the shrub. Multiple planters can be grouped as shown.

butted up tightly against each other; when complete, a 1 × 4 finishing strip is added around the perimeter.

For walkways, a simpler grid pattern is used. However, as shown in the photo at left, steps or different levels can be added by changing the joist height in certain areas.

Although Ajax originally designed the squares for decking, there are lots of other uses. For instance, four Deck Squares nailed together as a box make the planter shown. Four squares mounted on a base of tiered risers make a patio coffee table. The table can be surrounded with benches made of Deck Squares that are supported by a frame of 2 × 6s with 2 × 4 legs. Squares can even serve as a cover for a sandbox, as shown below. The box is made of 2 × 10s with an exterior-plywood base. (Be sure to drill a few drain holes for water in the base.)

Raised decks can be enclosed with squares mounted along the sides. With the addition of hinges and locking hardware, some squares (or groups of squares) become access doors for outdoor storage bins.

Deck Squares are available through local home-improvement stores.—*Text by William J. Hawkins*

Added touches: Deck Squares table, sandbox with cover (above), and flower boxes (below).

A striking basket-weave-pattern deck is formed by laying mahogany tiles in alternating directions. The square tiles are especially suited for building rectangular-shaped decks. For contrast cedar was used for risers and edge trim.

This deck sits on poured-concrete posts, but pressure-treated wood posts can also be used. Sheet-metal anchors secure the posts to the pressure-treated beams that support the 2×8 joists. These joists must be spaced on 12-inch centers instead of the more common 16-inch spacing.

20 Hardwood Tiles Make a Parquet Deck

"These new deck tiles are ideal for the do-it-yourselfer," says Chicago architect Tom Hood. "Each tile is finished, so no cutting or sanding is required."

Hood designed his 16-by-24-foot deck around two-foot-square Moore-Tile. The mahogany tiles are approximately 1-inch thick and consist of eight slats stapled to three backer slats. Because South American mahogany is such a dense wood, there is no splintering problem, and the tiles resist rot and insect damage.

At $14 a tile (at most home centers), this decking material costs about the same as redwood or pressure-treated lumber. But because of their size, the tiles are faster to install than standard decking. A Moore-Tile deck requires about 25 percent fewer fasteners than an equivalent-size plank deck. And it's easier to align 2-foot-sq. modules than it is to work with 6-foot-long planks.

The square tile has other advantages, according to Hood. He first planned his deck on graph paper, using 2-foot squares as basic building blocks. He found uses for the versatile tiles as stair treads, vertical skirting, and walkways.

"If you lay out your deck in 2-foot increments and use standard-size lumber, you have a minimum of cutting and waste," Hood says. He framed his deck in No. 2 pressure-treated lumber and used cedar rails and posts for trim.

The framework is the most difficult part of any deck. With Moore-Tile you can hire a carpenter to erect the framework (especially if your location is on a sloping site), but you can save money by laying the decking yourself. (Of course, before beginning any deck installation you should also check local building codes.)

Building the deck frame to support these tiles is done the

Fastening holes must be pre-drilled (above). Cedar shims can be wedged under tiles if joist surfaces are irregular. Tiles require a screw per corner, but only two screws per tile are needed to mount for skirting (right). Cedar trim hides exposed edges of tile.

Match tiles for color after cutting to make stair treads. Pre-drill to prevent splitting. Though cedar was used for risers here, tiles may be used instead.

For walkways in low-traffic areas, such as alongside house (right), tiles can be laid right atop gravel bed contained in frame of pressure-treated wood, as shown at left. For heavy-traffic areas excavate shallow trench to hold frame.

same way you'd construct a standard lumber deck—except for joist spacing. The ½-inch tile slats require a joist every 12 inches for support instead of the more common 16-inch-on-center spacing. (This means you need about 30 percent more lumber for the joists. But as a bonus you get a sturdier deck.)

If you want the tiles flush with the deck edge, allow 9¾ inches instead of 10½ inches between outer joists and the next joist. This adjustment will put the tile edge flush with the outside edge of the joist.

Installing the tiles is much like laying a tile floor except that you start along the outside edges of the deck instead of an inner wall. "Alternating tile direction creates a basket-weave pattern that hides minor errors," Hood says.

Lay the first tile at an outside corner, using a framing square. Then rough-lay the tiles along both edges of the deck. Trim tiles to fit when necessary. You can cut as much as needed when trimming the slats—but if you cut more than 3 inches across the slats, you'll cut off the backer slat. To keep slats in place while cutting, install a new backer slat inside the old one before you cut.

Moore-Tile can be nailed or screwed. "I found No. 8 1¾-inch brass flathead screws, bought in bulk at a hardware supplier, the most economical," says Hood. "We used 500 screws that cost around $50." The brass quickly tarnishes and blends in with the wood. Stainless-steel screws are a bit more expensive but will not tarnish with age like the brass.

Screw holes must be pre-drilled through the dense hardwood tile. Using two electric drills speeds the job. Keep a countersinking bit (Screwmate is a good one) in one for drilling the pilot holes, and a screwdriver bit in the other for quick installation of the four screws per tile.

Hood gave the deck tiles two coats of Thompson's Water Sealer, using a long-nap paint roller. One coat was applied before the tiles were laid, and the final coat was applied after the deck was completed.

What about maintenance? "If a deck is located under shade or sap trees, it's a good idea to remove leaves before winter to avoid discoloration," Hood says. "This happens on any type of decking but can be easily avoided."

The versatile tiles are suited for more than decking. Cut in half, they make stair treads. Stringer spacing is the same 12-inches-on-center as that of the joists. Tiles also can be laid vertically to make a deck skirting.

Moore-Tile is also suited for creating walkways and even

small patios. Because the mahogany tiles are rot resistant, they can be laid over a gravel bed or directly onto a plastic sheet if the walkway is not a high-traffic area.

For a walkway built on grade, use pressure-treated 2 × 4s—laid parallel and 24 inches apart—as a walkway frame. Hold the frame in place with wood stakes driven into the ground on the inside.

Nail 2-foot lengths of 2 × 4 across the frame at 4-foot intervals to hold the side rails parallel. Then place plastic between the 2 × 4s to hold back weeds. Fill with gravel, smoothing it to about 1-inch from the top of the 2 × 4s. Finally, insert the tiles, and backfill against the form if necessary.

The deck tiles have a variety of other uses, according to the importer (William G. Moore & Son Inc. of Delaware, 482 Manor Rd., Staten Island, N.Y. 10314-0008). The tiles can transform an urban "tar beach" into a handsome roof deck simply by applying flashing adhesive to the backer slats and pressing in place. The tiles can be screwed directly into a run-down existing deck, once loose and broken slats are nailed in place. Finally, the tiles can be glued atop an existing concrete or flagstone patio. Or they can be fitted into a perimeter frame attached to the patio.—*Text by Gene and Katie Hamilton.*

21 Bolt-Plate Shelters for Your Yard

It floats above the forest like a temple in a Chinese scroll. The Victorians would have labeled it a "folly"—their term for any fanciful structure (usually decorating a lawn or garden) that was built for other than sound practical purpose. Yet this folly can provide you with both outdoor shelter and out-of-season storage. And it's assembled with special steel connectors, called Starplates, that you can find at many home centers.

I hung my folly off a mountain to demonstrate—the hard way—that similar structures can be built anywhere, and I used the plates which let you bolt 2 × 4s into a sturdy web like a full-scale Erector set. How you cover your frame depends on the use the structure will serve. For a true folly, you could lattice the roof framing to provide a patterned shade; other possibilities are shown on page 138.

Because I wanted winter closure, I chose to nail lap siding on the lower half of the walls, wrapping the upper half in a special new black-coated aluminum screening. Shutters hinged to fold up inside, close the space from weather, and a large hinged panel at the front winches down for the spectacular view. In a backyard setting this panel could serve as a ramp for wheeling-in lawn mowers, carts, and bikes.

Was construction as easy as manufacturers of the assembly plates claim? Initially, yes. One promotion brochure promised a "two-hour frame-up." What this neglects to mention is that it may take several days to trim, drill, and sand the struts for assembly, and many days of tedious angle-cutting if you plan to apply plank siding or roof shingles. (I did both, and it took an entire summer's weekends.) Of course, I complicated the roofing even further by building where I had limited access and by piercing the roof with skylights.

Construction plans for the basic frame are sketched on page

A stamped steel plate has sockets that let you bolt together five identically drilled 2 × 4s to form the joints in the shelter.

This gazebo seems to float off the mountain. Its front panel has been winched down for maximum view. At bottom left, the triangular access panel is propped up for entry. At bottom right, the access and interior shutters are closed for winter.

134

GAZEBO OFF MOUNTAIN

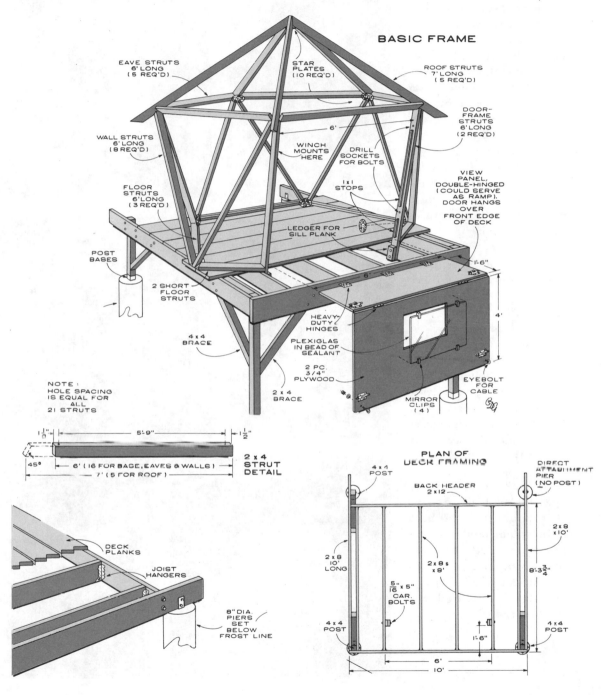

BASIC FRAME

EAVE STRUTS
6' LONG
(5 REQ'D)

STAR
PLATES
(10 REQ'D)

ROOF STRUTS
7' LONG
(5 REQ'D)

DOOR-
FRAME
STRUTS
6' LONG
(2 REQ'D)

6'

WALL STRUTS
6' LONG
(8 REQ'D)

WINCH
MOUNTS
HERE

DRILL
SOCKETS
FOR BOLTS

VIEW
PANEL,
DOUBLE-HINGED
(COULD SERVE
AS RAMP).
DOOR HANGS
OVER
FRONT EDGE
OF DECK

FLOOR
STRUTS
6' LONG
(3 REQ'D)

1 x 1
STOPS

POST
BASES

LEDGER FOR
SILL PLANK

1'-6"

2 SHORT
FLOOR
STRUTS

6'

4'

4 x 4
BRACE

HEAVY-
DUTY
HINGES

NOTE:
HOLE SPACING
IS EQUAL FOR
ALL
21 STRUTS

PLEXIGLAS
IN BEAD OF
SEALANT

2 PC.
3/4"
PLYWOOD

2 x 4
BRACE

MIRROR
CLIPS
(4)

EYEBOLT
FOR
CABLE

1½"

5'-9"

1½"

45°

6' (16 FOR BASE, EAVES & WALLS)

2 x 4
STRUT
DETAIL

7' (5 FOR ROOF)

**PLAN OF
DECK FRAMING**

4 x 4
POST

BACK HEADER
2 x 12

DIRECT
ATTACHMENT
PIER
(NO POST)

DECK
PLANKS

JOIST
HANGERS

2 x 8
10'
LONG

2 x 8 s
x 8'

2 x 8
x 10'

5/16" x 5"
CAR.
BOLTS

8'-3¾"

8" DIA.
PIERS
SET
BELOW
FROST LINE

4 x 4
POST

1'-6"

4 x 4
POST

6'

10'

To create metal anchor for corner that rests directly on pier, cut tubular form to exact height, wedge in position atop concrete footing, bolt scrap 2×4 between metal plates (with extra bolts through lower holes), lay across form, and fill to rim with concrete. Wait two days, remove 2×4, and save to use as template for drilling joist. Doubled outer joists flank 4×4 posts; to prevent racking, bolt 4×4 knee braces between (top right).

Placement of inner joists was eased with Teco hangers nailed to inner faces of front and back beams prior to erection. Redwood deck planks were nailed across joists so trial base frame, bolted to Starplates, could be centered on deck. Two side corners jutted beyond frame, so longer planks were installed there (center right).

With planking completed up to threshold, base struts at front are trimmed back to butt door jambs. Jambs pass through deck and bolt through framing; note that face block is needed to support threshold at each end (bottom right).

Four remaining Starplates are now anchored to deck. Top of each jamb bolts to inside of its plate (left). Extra 2×4s were added as supports for sheathing frames and a skylight (right).

 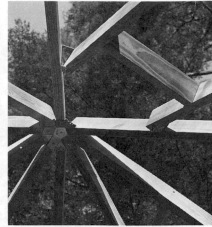

Triangular plywood panels were added for roof sheathing (left). Angle-cut pieces of lap siding (right) were anchored at each end with pairs of nails.

Removable interior shutters were made from plywood and waferboard (left). The viewing panel is shown being winched into the down position (right).

Adjusting size and skin to sheltering need

Three other Starplate shelters show system's versatility. Staple polyethylene film over frame (top) for a freestanding greenhouse that can be disassembled and stored during winter. Keep a sandbox dry by erecting a scaled-down shelter (middle). An ideal shed for lawn-and-garden-equipment storage is yours (bottom) if you cover all walls and hinge triangular plywood panels as lockable access doors.

135, along with step-by-step assembly photos that are packed with information. I had to erect a floating deck before I could start my gazebo (see pages 136 and 137 for photos). If you erect your structure on a flat yard, you're way ahead.

Prepare the 21 struts as shown in the sketch (pressure-treated lumber is best, especially for struts in ground contact). Assemble the five base struts, then erect eight wall struts and tie them together with the five eaves struts. To duplicate my square door frame, you'll have removed the two full-length base struts at the front corner to use elsewhere, replacing them with struts only long enough to butt against two vertical jambs that frame the opening. Unless you can bolt these jambs into a deck frame, as I did, you'll want to sink them into concrete footings.

You're now ready to proceed with the roof. In my case, the five-rafter frame is complicated with extra 2×4s to provide nailers for sheathing seams and framing for skylights; note the use of miter plates that the manufacturer added to the Starplate system to avoid compound-angle cuts. In one photo, I'm lifting half of a ½-inch CDX plywood sheet through the framing to nail in place (you can get two such right-angle triangles out of each 4-by-8-foot sheet). Once the sheathing was nailed on, I covered it with roofing felt and applied asphalt shingles. Because of inaccessibility from the ground, I did much of my shingling from a stepladder erected inside the structure, working out through the skylight openings, as shown in a photo.

A photo shows the tricky, wasteful angle-trimming required to apply lap siding. Planks are anchored to the frame with a pair of nails at each end; there's a 2×4 crosspiece behind the top edge of each top plank.

The interior shutters shown were made from ½-inch plywood or waferboard. The larger ones are hinged to eaves struts so they swing up against the ceiling when open. Smaller ones bolt in place; when removed, they store under the deck. The last photo shows the double-hinged view panel being winched down to hang over the deck's edge.—*Text and photos by Alfred Lees.*

SOURCES
Kant-Sag/United Steel Products, 703 Rogers Dr., Montgomery MN 56069. Starplate bolt plates, miter plates, roof cap;

Keystone-Seneca Wire Cloth Co., Box 386, Brookhaven MS 39601. Senaclad coated aluminum screening;

Teco Products, Colliers Way, Colliers, WV 26035. 4×4 post bases and joist hangers for deck

22 Bring Aging Decks Back to Life

Nature is ruthless. An unattended house will eventually rot and collapse; a car that is not cared for will rust and decay. The same holds true for the deck in your backyard. Unless you are unusually diligent, there will come a time when the effects of mold, mildew, and ultraviolet radiation will make your deck look worse for wear, and your elegant addition will become a weather-beaten blemish.

Until a few years ago there was not much you could do to keep your deck fresh looking, short of sanding it down or drenching it with a chlorine bleach or acid solution. Trouble was, sanding took a tremendous amount of effort—and often required resetting nailheads. Acids and bleach are toxic materials. They also give a deck a washed-out look. Enter wood renewers.

Wood renewers made especially for decks started surfacing four or five years ago. The first ones were acid- or bleach-based, but newer formulas kill mold and clean off gray tarnish to reveal fresh-looking wood without using acids or chlorine bleach. Of the half-dozen wood-renewing products now on the market, four are powders that are mixed with water; one is a concentrated solution that is diluted before use; and one is a liquid that's used full strength. Several experts in the field told me how and why wood weathers, how restorers work, what they are made of, what differences there are between them, and what you can do to keep your deck looking good once you have cleaned it.

"You've spent $3,000 to $5,000 on a deck," said Richard Tripodi, vice president of marketing for Darworth Co., "and now, three or four years later, it looks weather-beaten and is fast becoming an eyesore. What do you do?"

That was a major concern homeowners expressed to Darworth, manufacturer of Cuprinol wood preservatives and

139

Foam means this deck cleaner is working. After you spray it onto the deck and work it in with a broom, rinse with water.

stains, in a consumer survey taken a few years ago. "Nobody, including our company, thought too hard about maintenance before," Tripodi says. "Everyone was so hung up on new deck building that nobody was paying attention to what you do, say, three years down the road."

What precisely happens to wood exposed to the elements? According to Alan Ross, who holds a Ph.D. in organic chemistry and is technical director of protection products for Koppers Co., manufacturer of Wolman Deck Brightener, three things affect decks: Dirt settles on, gets grround into, and gets spilled on the wood; mildew and other organisms grow on the wood's surface, darkening it; and ultraviolet radiation breaks down the surface cellulose cells, making them go gray. Any product that is going to rejuvenate weathered wood effectively must attack these three problems.

"Historically, the most common substance used to clean

wood has been a sodium hypochlorite or calcium hypochlorite material like household bleach," Ross told me. "Those materials will remove mildew, but they leave behind degraded cellulose cells and give the wood a washed-out appearance. Also, they are toxic to plants.

"Another common material is oxalic acid, which is particularly good at dissolving tannin resins. It's effective on redwood, which is notorious for tannin secretion," Ross went on. "Oxalic acid does not really do anything for mildew or dirt. What it does remove are dark tannin stains."

One of the first of the wood restorers was Dekswood, a concentrated liquid from The Flood Co. that is based on a solution of detergents and 10 percent oxalic acid. I tried it on a small area of weathered redwood, spraying it on, rubbing it in with a stiff brush, then rinsing it off. It cleaned the redwood well. A newer product, also a liquid, is Macklanburg-Duncan's Weather Warrior, a solution based on the chlorine bleach sodium hypochlorite and cupric hydroxide, an acid. Some of its label warnings include "May discolor clothing," "Avoid contact with plants," and "Wear gloves."

The newest wood-rejuvenating products are the four powders, Wolman Deck Brightener, Cuprinol Revive Deck Cleaner, Zar Wood Brightener, and Osmose Wood Brite. They are all based on the active ingredient sodium percarbonate. (You'll see other names on the labels, like disodium peroxydicarbonate, percarbonate of soda, and sodium carbonate peroxyhydrate. According to Ross, they are different chemical names for the same substance.)

"Sodium percarbonate is used in some denture cleaners, and is similar to what detergent people call nonchlorine bleach, or oxygen bleach," Ross says. "It relies on oxygen rather than chlorine to do the cleaning, and is not as caustic or reactive with colored materials like fabrics—or wood pigment."

In fact, the difference between a sodium percarbonate-based cleaner and a sodium hypochlorite-based one can be likened to the difference between an all-fabric bleach and a chlorine bleach: One enhances color while the other bleaches color out.

"After the powder is mixed and sprayed or mopped onto the deck," Ross explained, "the sodium percarbonate foams and breaks down into two chemicals, hydrogen peroxide and sodium carbonate. The hydrogen peroxide softens and helps remove the upper gray cell layers of the wood; sodium carbonate, which is perhaps better known as soda ash and is found in baking powder, baking soda, and soaps, acts as a cleaner. After

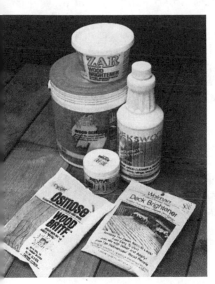

Six deck rejuvenators banish gray better than Grecian Formula: Zar Wood Brightener, Weather Warrior Wood Restorer, Flood Dekswood, Cuprinol Revive, Osmose Wood Brite (left foreground), Wolman Deck Brightener.

141

SOURCES:
Darworth Co., 50 Tower Lane, Avon CT 06001; The Flood Co., Box 399, Hudson OH 44236; Koppers Co., 436 Seventh Ave., Pittsburgh PA 15219; Macklan-burg-Duncan, Box 25188, Oklahoma City OK 73125-0188; Osmose Wood Products, Drawer O, Griffin GA 30224; United Gilsonite Laboratories, Box 70, Scranton PA 18501

you let the solution stand on the wood for about 10 minutes, you go over the deck with a stiff-bristle broom, then rinse it off with water. The effect is not unlike what you'd get if you were to plane the wood to get an extremely fine veneer off its surface."

Although the powders all contain some form of sodium carbonate, there are subtle differences among them, primarily in some of their cleaning agents. For example, John Molski, United Gilsonite Laboratories' technical director, told me Zar Wood Brightener uses sodium metasilicate and sodium perborate, along with sodium sesquicarbonate, as cleaners. "We did about two years of testing, using exposure panels as well as actual weathered decks, to come up with the right combination of cleaning power and safe use."

Now that you've cleaned your deck, how do you keep it looking good?

"Depending on the effect you want," Darworth's Tripodi answered, "you can use a semi-transparent stain and wood preservative or a clear wood sealer. A stained finish will give you just about any color you want. A solid stain is not recommended, however, because you won't see much of the wood's grain and the finish will wear noticeably in high-traffic areas. A semi-transparent stain will enhance the grain effect, and the finish will probably last for two or three years. A clear sealer will not last as long as a stained finish. It should be reapplied annually. A water-based clear sealer is easy to apply: You can just spray it on with a garden sprayer."

No matter what you do, you won't completely eliminate the ravages of time. But with a little care and the right equipment, you can soften its blow and keep your deck beautiful.—*Text by Timothy O. Bakke.*

23 Gazebos to Go

The date of the wedding was rapidly approaching. Robert Gedney's daughter was getting married and he wanted someplace special to hold the ceremony, but nothing that came to mind seemed appropriate. Then about a month before the ceremony he had the idea of erecting a gazebo from a kit. Both the airy garden structure he built in his backyard and the wedding ceremony were a smashing success.

The gazebo is not only a natural focal point for landscaping, but a pleasant open-air spot for entertaining or relaxing. The word "gazebo" probably comes from the combination of "gaze" and the latin ending *ebo,* as in *videbo* (I shall see).

From The English Garden kit's arrival to the completed free-standing garden structure, assembly of the 8½-foot octagonal gazebo requires two people and no more than five hours, says David Kettlewell, who imports his gazebo kits from England. "Construction can easily be done on a weekend day," he claims. "All parts are pre-cut and pre-drilled, and there is no special training or knowledge of carpentry needed."

The astounding variety of build-it-yourself gazebos ranges from a 7-foot-square model to a 35-foot octagonal behemoth. Prices start at less than $2,000 for a small square gazebo unit to $35,000 for a bandstand that would top off a new park.

Assembly of the typical polygonal gazebo is mapped out with an instruction booklet. You start by preparing a secure base, says Douglas Jefferys, vice president of Vixen Hill Gazebos. Pressure-treated timbers sunk into the ground—or better yet, a poured concrete foundation—will do just fine. Next you arrange the kiosk's floor joists in a spoke pattern and bolt them to the footings. Then attach the triangular floor sections. The next phase of construction—putting up the ceiling supports—

143

SOURCES:

Advanced Spa Designs, 1311 Blue Gum, Anaheim CA 92806; Cumberland Woodcraft Co., Drawer 609, Carlisle PA 17013; Dalton Pavilions, 7260-68 Oakley St., Philadelphia PA 19111; The English Garden, 652 Glenbrook Rd., Stamford CT 06906; Gazebo Nostalgia, 1780 Magnolia Way, Walnut Creek CA 94595; Vintage Wood Works, 513 S. Adams, Fredericksburg TX 78624; Vixen Hill Gazebos, Maine and Railroad Tracks, Elverson PA 19520

requires two people. After erecting the supports, ring the framework with railing at the floor level and fit the molding to the rails.

While most kits use wood roofs, The English Garden gazebos have lightweight fiberglass tops, tinted gray to look like lead. Kettlewell says that this type of roof is nearly indestructible, "except if a tree falls on it or it is shot with a rifle." Whether made of wood in sections or as a one-piece fiberglass unit, the roof is positioned and locked into place. A roof cupola, weather vane, or interior lighting completes the project.

What's the major reason for the recent resurgence of these outdoor edifices? "By its nature the gazebo brings some of the comforts of indoors to the great outdoors," says Jefferys. Many of these garden retreats have a minimal structure, with wooden slats for a roof or latticework and a trellis making up the walls; others take the gazebo to another level.

The deluxe line built by Advanced Spa Designs features 1×3 redwood slats that have been turned to dowels and arranged so that the sun can stream in. The company's 8-foot-square unit takes the garden-room concept a step further: It is designed to fit over most hot tubs.

The English Garden makes a glassed-in gazebolike English summerhouse with a fish-scale-pattern solid roof and windows that swing open. The glass gazebo can easily double as an office or summer house. A glazed gazebo also overcomes the problem of outdoor insect pests during the summer.

You don't go for glass? Glenn Dalton, of Dalton Pavilions, says in that case the answer is a screened-in gazebo. "We sell many screened-in gazebos for use in areas where it would be difficult to sit outside in the evening and enjoy yourself without being bitten."

While many people choose to leave the wooden surface natural, some paint their gazebos. One artistically inclined gazebo owner in San Francisco applied a two-tone paint job, reminiscent of the gazebo's Victorian roots.

Although the gazebo may speak of a different age, these pavilions are built to modern standards, and pass all building codes. I was astonished by the variety of styles and shapes available to the handy homeowner searching for a backyard focal point. With many accessories available to customize these garden rooms, there should be a gazebo that suits every house.—*Text by Brian Nadel.*

The gazebo continues to develop: Glass sides and door turn the traditional gazebo into a mini-greenhouse/sun room on the lawn (above).

Adding doors and screens allows you to enjoy your outdoor room in comfort (right).

II Sunspaces, Sun Porches, Sun Rooms

From modest bump-outs to opulent additions, sunspaces are today's hottest home improvement—bringing the outdoors in and making any home brighter and bigger. Although you can build your own unit from scratch, there is also a broad choice of kits available. Can you erect them yourself? What do they cost? Should the support frame be wood or metal? What type of glazing is best for your site? Which side of the house should they attach to—and which room? Will they be too cold in winter and too hot in summer? The following pages will help you decide which sunspace is right for your home, whether you should tackle the job yourself, and how to choose from the glazing options and accessories now available. And if you think a sunspace gives your home *too* much exposure, here's a selection of sun porches and sun rooms as well.

24 Do-It-Yourself Add-On Lean-To

Northeast winters tend to be cold and gray. But the sun-drenched room I designed and added to my home has changed that. It's a warm, bright add-on, suitable as a breakfast room, for simply relaxing with a book, or for hot-tubbing in a whirlpool tub I've installed. As I write this in midwinter, a small fan is quietly blowing 80-degree-F air from the sunspace into my house.

This project called for inexpensive, readily obtained materials and do-it-yourself building techniques, since I planned to do most of the construction. Also, I wanted to use the space both summer and winter, but with minimal shading or insulation.

A 60-degree sloped bank of windows can be ideal for capturing the winter sun. However, combine that with a vertical knee wall (for ventilation) and a sloped roof (to shed water), and you have an unstable configuration. To solve this problem I designed a structural system of prefabricated plywood ribs. Located at the glazing joints, they provide both roof structure and window mullion.

Snug interior of add-on sunspace during winter months is aided by fiberglass insulation for the floor and ceiling, plus moderate thermal storage mass to capture solar energy streaming through large, sloped windows during the day. The outdoor platform for a 195-gallon whirlpool spa (middle left) sits on a leveled gravel bed. During winter months, this portable spa can be moved inside the sunspace (bottom left). Architect Milstein decided to glaze one end wall for a nice view (far right), leaving other wall solid except for a low awning to catch westerly summer breezes. Quarry-tile floor over concrete stores solar heat.

ADD-ON LEAN-TO

OPENINGS
FRAMING DETAIL

Simple wooden frame, left, added to any existing south wall supports both the solid, insulated roof (with openings framed for skylight and two turbine vents) and angled double glazing. Full plans are available (see last page).

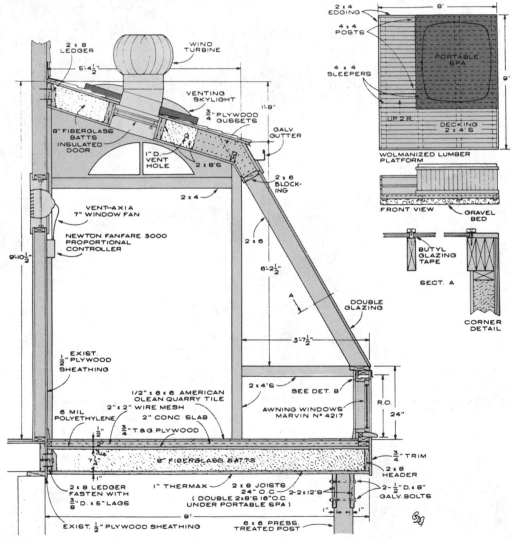

2 x 8 LEDGER

WIND TURBINE

5'-4½"

VENTING SKYLIGHT

1'-8"

¾" PLYWOOD GUSSETS

GALV. GUTTER

8" FIBERGLASS BATTS INSULATED DOOR

1" D. VENT HOLE

2 x 8'S

2 x 6 BLOCKING

2 x 4

VENT-AXIA 7" WINDOW FAN

2 x 6

NEWTON FANFARE 3000 PROPORTIONAL CONTROLLER

9'-10½"

6'-2½"

A

DOUBLE GLAZING

3'-7½"

EXIST. ½" PLYWOOD SHEATHING

1/2" x 6 x 6 AMERICAN OLEAN QUARRY TILE

2" x 2" WIRE MESH

2" CONC. SLAB

¾" T. & G. PLYWOOD

2 x 4'S

SEE DET. B

AWNING WINDOWS MARVIN N° 4217

R.O.

24"

6 MIL POLYETHYLENE

½"

2"

7¼"

1"

8" FIBERGLASS BATTS

¾" TRIM

2 x 8 HEADER

2 x 8 LEDGER FASTEN WITH ⅜" D. x 6" LAGS

1" THERMAX

2 x 8 JOISTS 24" O.C. (DOUBLE 2 x 8'S 16" O.C. UNDER PORTABLE SPA)

2-2 x 12'S

2-½" D. x 8" GALV. BOLTS

1"   1"

9'

EXIST. ½" PLYWOOD SHEATHING

6 x 6 PRESS. TREATED POST

2 x 4 EDGING

8'

4 x 4 POSTS

PORTABLE SPA

9'

4 x 4 SLEEPERS

UP 2 R.

DECKING 2 x 4 6

WOLMANIZED LUMBER PLATFORM

FRONT VIEW

GRAVEL BED

BUTYL GLAZING TAPE

SECT. A

CORNER DETAIL

150

Pouring and smoothing cubic yard of concrete (left) took an hour. After striking off excess flush with form (as shown) finish surface with bull float. Half-inch quarry tiles atop 2-inch concrete slab create thermal storage mass. Bed them in a thin-set mortar.

Ribs are formed with plywood gussets glued and nailed across the joint on each face. Use waterproof glue. Inside finishes for the sunspace are ½-inch gypsum board on the wall and ceiling. A 6-foot-wide door opens into the house.

Simple wooden frame, left, added to any existing south wall supports both the solid, insulated roof (with openings framed for skylight and two turbine vents) and angled double glazing. Full plans are available (see last page).

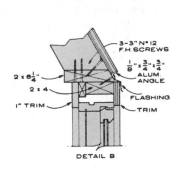

3-3" N°12 F.H SCREWS

⅛" ¾" ¾" ALUM. ANGLE

2 x 6¼"

2 x 4

1" TRIM

FLASHING

TRIM

DETAIL B

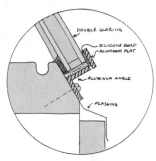

DOUBLE GLAZING

SILICONE BEAD

ALUMINUM FLAT

ALUMINUM ANGLE

FLASHING

ATTACH A CONTINUOUS STRIP OF ⅛" x ⅝" (OR ¾") ALUMINUM FLAT STOCK, USING BEADS OF SILICONE SPACED AT APPROX. 2'O.C. AS AN ADHESIVE. THIS IS TO PROTECT THE SEALANT ON THE GLAZING UNIT FROM THE SUN'S ULTRAVIOLET WHICH CAN DEGRADE THE SEALANT AND CAUSE A FAILURE OF THE GLAZING SEAL

Note: The sketches are only intended to help you evaluate this project. To order large-format plans, including clear construction details, sources for materials, plans for an insulating night shade, and building hints, send $25 to: Jeff Milstein, P.O. Box 172, Woodstock, N.Y. 12498. Allow 4 to 6 weeks delivery. New York State residents add sales tax. The plans have not been updated so source addresses may not be current, but construction details are thorough and complete.

An insulated roof helps keep the sunspace warm in winter and cool in summer. A 2–inch–thick concrete floor slab covered with ½-inch quarry tile provides some thermal mass to store solar heat. To maximize solar heat for direct warming of adjacent areas of your house, you should keep thermal mass to this minimum. But to retain most heat *within* the sunspace—say, for growing plants—you may want a greater storage mass.

Natural ventilation for summer is important. Awning windows are installed along the floor perimeter, and two 14-inch-diameter wind turbines and a venting skylight are on the roof. Insulated, weatherstripped doors were built to seal off the turbine vents in the winter. On winter nights, I close the double French doors between the house and sunspace, allowing the outer temperature to drop into the 40's.

To control the sunspace environment, I've installed a window fan in the wall between the sunspace and the house. A special control for the fan has a low setting that protects plants from freezing by blowing heat from the house on unusually cold nights. Another setting blows warm air into the house on sunny days. A solid-state circuit automatically varies fan speed with demand.

A 10-foot-by-10-foot-by-8-inch concrete-block Trombe wall existed on the side of my house before I began the sunspace. After the glazing this also became thermal storage mass. Unless you have a masonry house, a similar heat storage probably isn't available to you. But the equivalent thermal storage is possible with about thirty cubic feet of water in containers placed in direct sunlight against the wall.

Selecting the glazing material was easy: The 46-inch-by-76-inch (or 34 inch by 76 inch) insulated, tempered, sliding patio-door replacements I used are the most economical double glazing I could find. I bought them for less than $80 each by shopping around. Although low-iron glass would transmit more light into the sunspace, I found it was expensive and hard to find.—*Text, photos and small sketch by Jeff Milstein.*

25 Double-Sunspace Addition

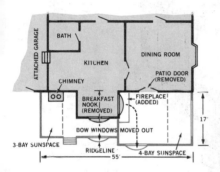

ATTACHED GARAGE

BATH

KITCHEN

CHIMNEY

DINING ROOM

PATIO DOOR (REMOVED)

BREAKFAST NOOK (REMOVED)

FIREPLACE (ADDED)

BOW WINDOWS MOVED OUT

17'

3-BAY SUNSPACE

RIDGELINE

55'

4-BAY SUNSPACE

See color photo on page 146.

When a homeowner in Brewster, N.Y., decided to expand a little breakfast-nook projection from his south-facing rear wall, he knew he wanted to incorporate a kit sunspace into a side wall. But he couldn't decide which side, so he ended up ordering a kit for both. Because these units had to be custom-made to fit the framing of the new wing, he contacted Solar Additions, a sunspace company that's well-known for working with homeowners. (See source list at end of chapter.)

Solar Additions had just introduced a new "window room" it calls Nature's Window. Basically, it's a 4-foot-deep, 9-foot-high extension with 46-by-76-inch window bays (three, four, five, or more) set vertically between laminated arches of either yellow pine or redwood.

The completed interior of this homeowner's three-bay Nature's Window is shown in the photo that opens this sunspace section. Exterior shots show both the three- and four-bay units. Photos of other applications of such a unit are shown at the end of the chapter.

To order a kit tailored to your needs you send a photo or sketch of your home's south-facing wall to Solar Additions. Its designers respond with design sketches and estimates. When you buy the custom-made unit it arrives in pieces with instructions for assembly. (Or the company will help you find a qualified local contractor.)

Often you'll have to cut out a section of the wall where Nature's Window will be spliced on; but in the case of the Brewster house, the kit frames were simply tied into the wall and roof framing for the new wing. The new roofing was extended down over the insulated roof deck of the sunspaces at both eaves. (Solar Additions recommends a venting skylight for each bay, but this feature is optional.) Once the new siding was applied, the kits all but disappeared when viewed from the exterior.

DOUBLE SUNSPACE

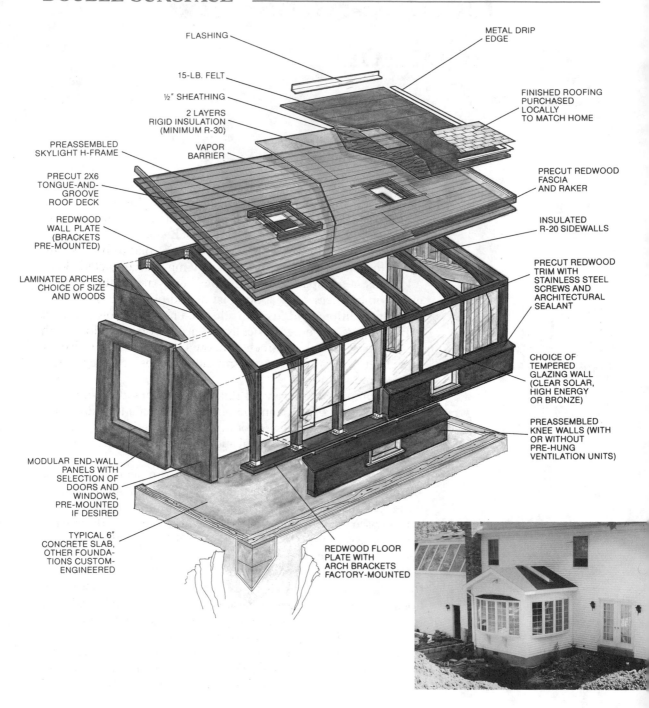

FLASHING

METAL DRIP EDGE

15-LB. FELT

½" SHEATHING

2 LAYERS RIGID INSULATION (MINIMUM R-30)

FINISHED ROOFING PURCHASED LOCALLY TO MATCH HOME

PREASSEMBLED SKYLIGHT H-FRAME

VAPOR BARRIER

PRECUT 2X6 TONGUE-AND-GROOVE ROOF DECK

PRECUT REDWOOD FASCIA AND RAKER

REDWOOD WALL PLATE (BRACKETS PRE-MOUNTED)

INSULATED R-20 SIDEWALLS

LAMINATED ARCHES, CHOICE OF SIZE AND WOODS

PRECUT REDWOOD TRIM WITH STAINLESS STEEL SCREWS AND ARCHITECTURAL SEALANT

CHOICE OF TEMPERED GLAZING WALL (CLEAR SOLAR, HIGH ENERGY OR BRONZE)

PREASSEMBLED KNEE WALLS (WITH OR WITHOUT PRE-HUNG VENTILATION UNITS)

MODULAR END-WALL PANELS WITH SELECTION OF DOORS AND WINDOWS, PRE-MOUNTED IF DESIRED

TYPICAL 6" CONCRETE SLAB, OTHER FOUNDATIONS CUSTOM-ENGINEERED

REDWOOD FLOOR PLATE WITH ARCH BRACKETS FACTORY-MOUNTED

Exterior view of the three-bay sunspace shows the unit built into the house addition—an option possible because the manufacturer customizes each order. Upper domed skylights were added by the owner.

The photo at left shows the original projection from the back wall of this two-story tract house—a cramped breakfast nook with two bow windows that received little direct sun. As shown in the floor plan (page 153) and in the photo on the right, the owner expanded the projection from the existing ridge line and incorporated a sunspace at both eaves.

155

How to site a sunspace

The survey map of your lot will show true north and south, but might not show how your house is oriented. If you site with a compass, you may have to apply a correction of as much as 23 degrees. (Compass and true south agree only on a line through Michigan and Florida.) Once you've found true south you can determine the area that should be free of obstructions. Use compass or protractor to locate 60 degrees east and west of true south as seen from your intended site. These are the points where the sun rises and sets in midwinter. Most solar heat is gained between the time from about 45 degrees east of south (9 a.m. solar time) to 45 degrees west (3 p.m.), so obstructions outside this zone are no problem. Floorplan sketches show best ways to position a sunspace.
—*John H. Mauldin*

Mauldin is a designer-builder of solar structures and the author of Sunspaces—Home Additions for Year-Round Natural Living *($14.60 paperback; Tab Books, Blue Ridge Summit, PA 17294-0859), from which sketches at upper right have been adapted.*

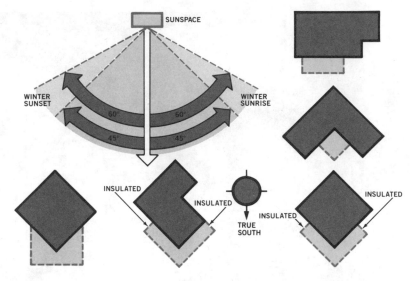

They were absorbed into the general structure of this extension.

But that aspect of this project is atypical. It's more common for kits of this type to be spliced onto a south-facing wall of a living room, bedroom, or kitchen. The erection procedure is basically the same—and basically as simple. I watched the complete four-bay unit in Brewster go up in one day with a crew of three.

The unit must sit on its own foundation, poured or concrete block. The floor can be an insulated slab or subflooring over wood joists. Either way, you'll probably want to face it with ceramic tile to provide a heat-absorbing masonry mass.

No flooring material comes with the kit, which does include the laminated arches, the ledger and floor plates these arches span, glass, the roofing system, all required fasteners, hardware, and redwood trim. Options include the operable skylights and sun screens.

As the assembly photos indicate, erection isn't especially tricky because, as with most other factory-made kits, parts are designed to fit together. The critical starting point is checking that the redwood floor plate and wall plate are precisely parallel, because each comes with brackets already mounted at the proper spacing to take the laminated arches that bridge these brackets to support the glazing. If the plates diverge from parallel, some arches will be too long or too short.

You run two continuous parallel beads of silicone sealant along the full width of the subfloor before setting the floor plate

After floor plate with pre-mounted brackets is anchored to foundation's sill plate, laminated arches are tipped in place [1] and drilled through bracket holes at top [2] and bottom; then they're bolted in place. Holes for skylights (one per bay) are cut through tongue-and-groove roof deck [3]. Note that deck is recessed below sheathing of adjacent structure to accommodate rigid insulation. Final sheathing on unit—for nailing on shingles—will set flush with adjacent roof. Vertical glass is tipped into rabbets in frame [4]. Note sealed edge of the double glazing.

in place. The wall plate may have to be notched into the siding or shimmed out. Do a neat job because it remains visible after assembly.

Next, insert the preassembled kneewall panels, sealing all joints and anchoring the frames to the arches. At our site the bottom frames of these panels hadn't been factory-notched to clear the bolt heads securing the arch brackets, so a router came in handy. Insert header strips between the hips of the arches, then add the end walls. You can opt for these solid panels to be factory-assembled. We put ours together on site.

Now nail the tongue-and-groove 2 × 6s across the arches to form a roof deck. And if you've chosen the skylight option, cut a rough opening centered on each bay for which a skylight has been supplied. Staple 4-mil polyethylene (a vapor barrier) over the roof deck, then cut out the holes for the skylights and install the preassembled H frames, centering them around the sky-

157

Year-round swimming is one benefit of this 39-foot-long pool enclosure customized by Solar Additions for Russell and Beverly Dunham of Danbury, CT. The 18-foot-deep addition, with the slanting solar windows sited south, captures winter sun and keeps it inside. Skylights and end doors open for ventilation on warm days. A long, skinny solar lean-to is an ideal enclosure for a narrow lap pool installed along a foundation wall.

A wasted corner in the L-shaped Colonial home of Dr. Ralph Stroup in Orange, CT was enclosed by this Solar Additions structure (right). Here the laminated arches are installed upright, with two of them meeting at a support post, to turn the outer corner with glazing. The 14 feet of four-foot-deep bays provide solar heat on winter days, but the space is a cozy joy in any season, ideal for informal parties.

light holes. Cover the whole deck with rigid insulation, notching it to fit snugly around the projections from the H frames. After dropping in the skylights, apply head and bottom flashing.

In our project the tongue-and-groove roof deck butted against the ends of the 2 × 6 rafters of the main structure. When we nailed on the ½-inch plywood sheathing (as a base for shingling) it came flush with the sheathing on the main roof. We drove 5-inch ring nails down through the rigid insulation and into the 2 × 6 decking.

To install the glass, run an unbroken bead of the silicone caulk around the redwood casing and set in the double-glazed panel. Hold it temporarily in place with the blocking provided. Fill all voids between the panel edges and casing with silicone. Next day, install the redwood trim supplied.

The order in which you tackle these steps may vary. You'll note in the photos that we installed the vertical glazing before dropping in the skylights. This gave us more flexibility in handling the big, heavy panels of glass (a three-person job) because we could pop up—or down—through the open roof holes. Roofing the entire structure with fiberglass shingles over 15-pound roofing felt was the final job.

What's the difference between these add-on sunspaces and the old shed greenhouses? "Energy management," says Lee

Stanley, pioneer sunspace designer and director of Solar Additions. "These units—installed for less than a new car would cost—are designed to tap solar energy for human comfort. And though you can certainly grow flowers and food in them all winter, they're meant as added living space. So they must be engineered for efficiencies well beyond those required by a greenhouse. Our models feature double glazing plus insulated roof and side walls to allow storage of solar heat in winter. They're ventilated to prevent overheating in summer. It's this kind of comfort that explains why over 150,000 sunspaces have been added to U.S. homes in the past decade, and why this is one of the best ways to upgrade a house for resale."

You can't just tack a sunspace onto any wall, however. These units should be oriented within 30 degrees of true south (see box on page 156). So how does this project manage a sunspace on both ends of the south-facing extension? By compromising proper siting.

A sunspace that doesn't face south can be a net loss as far as heat is concerned. If it's not in direct winter sun, not only will it fail to contribute any solar gain, it can be a big heat loser—unless you equip it with elaborate insulating drapes or shutters (see "Outfitting Your Sunspace"). And that could cancel out the main reason for installing a sunspace: to open up your home to outdoor views.

I asked John Mauldin (author of the box) which compromise was best when a *corner* of a house points true south, and it's impractical to wrap a sunspace around it. Do you add the unit to the wall angled east or west?

Mauldin told me his advice would depend on local weather patterns and family lifestyle. "Are winter mornings overcast or foggy while afternoons tend to be clear?" he asked. "Then your orientation should favor the west. Do you like an early-morning warmup and perhaps a cozy breakfast in the sunspace? Or will you use it for unwinding late in the day—maybe with a spa soak?"

The Brewster homeowner has a choice. The "morning" sunspace gets direct sun earlier and longer, so its position off the kitchen makes it a good breakfast nook. The "evening" sunspace gets less sun, later, so it sports only three bays and is comfortable for cocktails.

But if you must settle for only one, you'll be happiest with a sunspace you've tailored to your site, lifestyle, and local weather.—*Text by Alfred Lees, photos by Geoffrey Gross and the author, drawings by Mitchell J. Albala.*

SOURCES:
Solar Additions, P.O. Box 241, Greenwich, NY 12834 (Nature's Window sunspace); American Olean Tile Co., 1000 Cannon Ave., Lansdale PA 19446 (8-inch hex Primitive Encore ceramic floor tile: 811 Almond); Barcalounger, 6900 Six Forks Rd., Raleigh NC 27609 (Hot Lines wicker furniture in honey pecan finish: modular seating and occasional tables).

159

26 Expand Your Kitchen with a Sunspace

"**T**he job of a kitchen designer isn't just placing boxes along walls," Jim Krengel told our symposium. That remark grabbed me. I've long thought that identical cabinets marching around a room interrupted only by same-size appliances offer about as much visual interest as a long train of boxcars clattering past a railroad crossing.

I cornered Krengel—who was about to be elected president of the National Kitchen and Bath Assn.—after his lecture and commissioned him to tackle a kitchen remodel especially for *Popular Science*. "What we'd like," I told him, "is a kitchen for two cooks, zoned so their work areas don't overlap. We'll assume it's used by a two-career couple who share meal-preparation and party-hosting tasks. But the kitchen should also function for other combinations, such as a mother and teenager."

"I'll start with a standard kitchen that has a dinette and snack bar—say a room about 14×21 feet," Krengel proposed. "But double zoning eats up floorspace, and I doubt any homeowner will want to sacrifice the dinette or bar. So where do I get the extra space?"

"Jim, let's punch through the wall next to the sink and splice a commercial sunspace on the outside. Make the kitchen flow right into it—and make it a daylight breakfast room, with other functions."

Krengel agreed, warming to the challenge: "A sunspace can be dramatic after dark, too—especially if there's outdoor lighting of the trees or garden beyond. This assignment can involve several of my favorite themes: You'll want multi-height work surfaces so cooks of different sizes can find one that's comfortable for the chore at hand. I can also vary heights of the wall cabinets. And—best of all—I can build in two of everything!"

"Hers-and-his sinks, grills and microwaves," I began.

160

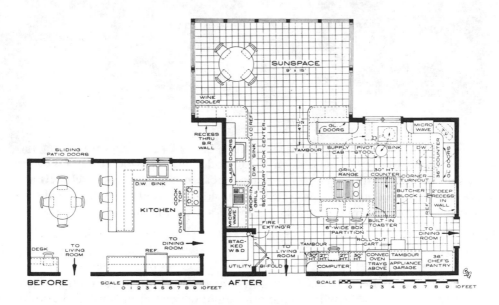

Before and after floor plans (above) show how tacking the sunspace onto the existing kitchen and eliminating the snack bar opens up the space. The new design provides room for both a serving and a cleanup zone, not to mention two cooks.

"And double dishwashers!" Jim added. "Makes sense if one dishwasher is in the food–preparation area and the other is across the kitchen in the serving-and-clean-up zone. That way, when loads are done, pots and pans go right into cabinets near the main stove and sink, while glassware, flatware and dishes go into cabinets where they'd be handy for setting the table."

Once Krengel had submitted his floorplan, I could see his logic. I saw it, too, in such unconventional appliance placement as the main oven across the room, next to the computer desk (see floorplan). Though this is the big oven, it's not necessarily the most-visited one. Things you put in a conventional oven have long baking or roasting times. You needn't make frequent check trips. On the other hand, the microwave is smack in the center of the food–preparation zone. And it's at a convenient height—achieved by setting the oven on a raised counter atop the dishwasher—which is also lifted by installing it on a platform. This means less bending to get heavy pots and pans in and out.

When I proposed the sunspace, I'd suggested that any wall cabinets that projected into its opening should have glass doors on *both* sides to let sunlight through. This offers ideal display storage for fine glassware.

Touches such as these are one reason for working with a CKD (certified kitchen designer) like Jim—and with a custom cabi-

161

Within the sunspace, the tinted glass door of the undercounter wine cooler (above) lets you check what's available but still cuts down on solar exposure. Note key in model's left hand: Unit locks to prevent unwanted use. An exercycle is a fine addition, and the light's ideal for reading while you ride. Or you may prefer to watch the TV set on the shelf below the wraparound countertop.

netmaker. Jim and I chose Wood-Mode Cabinetry, a factory that distributes nationally and which not only made all our counters and wall units to precise order, but which also furnished prefinished natural beech moldings around the wall cabinets and built-in appliances.

We invited DuPont to supply its Corian countertop throughout. Their fabricator did a skillful job of softening all edges and running a light-tan stripe just inside them. These edges were bulked up with a second strip of the 3/4-inch Corian, 2½ inches wide, bonded along the underside; the special Corian adhesive becomes invisible once the joint is sanded. The feature stripe was created by routing a shallow channel and filling it with the bonding adhesive. Once this set, the bead was sanded flush with the surface.

This feature stripe shows best in the photos of the model taken *inside* the sunspace. Note how Krengel has wrapped the counters into the sunspace at each side of the opening, and placed additional cabinets and shelves in this space, handy to the dinette. He's even tucked an electric wine cooler here, ready for evening entertaining. The cabinets can store games, with a compact TV stowed on one of the open shelves for viewing while using the exercycle. One of the joys of a sunspace is that it caters to outdoor activities on days when the weather doesn't.

The roll-out Wood-Mode cart that's garaged in the main-oven wall (not shown except in the floorplan) is ideal for sunspace service. You can load it with all breakfast needs and roll it to the table. Or just position it as an extra work counter anywhere it's needed in the kitchen.

Two food preparation zones keep cooks out of each other's way. His undercounter fridge is handy to the sunspace. Major fridge/freezer (far right) is within easy reach of her work island.

Dual dishwashers? It makes sense in a two-cook kitchen—especially after a party, as shown at right. One is in the serving and cleanup zone. The other, in the food-preparation zone is already full of pots, pans, and dishes used to prepare the meal. These Maytag units feature quiet operation so two running at once won't drive you out of the kitchen.

Entire secondary work zone flows into the sunspace dinette at rear. That add-on makes this spacious kitchen possible and even allows for a stacked washer/dryer behind folding doors (far left).

To splice a sunspace onto your kitchen, consult a reputable manufacturer of such units (see chart further along in this book) to learn what's involved in the removal of part of a wall. Our opening is nearly 12 feet across, so it required the addition of a laminated beam to bridge the gap in the framing. This becomes even more critical, of course, in a two-story house. The height of our redwood sunspace unit was customized to match the kitchen's 8-foot ceiling. The exterior height of the back wall is 6 feet 11 inches. A finished foundation measuring 9 feet 4 inches by 15 feet 5 inches was tied into the existing house foundation to take the weight of this double-glazed structure.

The kitchen island is made up of three custom cabinets bolted together to flank a slide-in range with an added structure of ¾-inch plywood to support a snack bar. One of the kitchen's finest design features is the stepped lighting valance that echoes in reverse the island's various planes—as if it were a lifted lid of that box. The range's down-draft feature eliminates any need for an exhaust hood overhead.

Strip lights above and below the wall cabinets and a fluorescent fixture above the sink window, plus recessed floorlights and spotlights in the ceiling provide adequate lighting at all work surfaces. All in all, America's CKD of the year designed us the kitchen of the year. And Krengel was able to pack in all these features because of the area gained by splicing on that handsome sunspace.—*Text by Alfred Lees, photos by Carl Shuman.*

27 Adding a Sunspace—Fast

Conservatories, sun rooms, greenhouses, solaria: They're all names for the glass-walled rooms, usually aluminum-framed but sometimes made of laminated wood, that have become increasingly popular among homeowners. These structures—with their prefabricated parts, integral insulation, and appealing styling—are economical, attractive additions to any house, new or old.

As an engineer, I'm interested in sunspace technology, so I jumped at a chance to watch Tom Nova of Energy Shield Systems erect a sun room. Nova and two other experienced workers were installing it on a house under construction in Dover, Vt., but they'd use the same materials and techniques to put up additions to existing houses.

The glass room that Nova built is a bit larger than the one pictured above; both are made by Sunplace, Inc., of Hinesburg, Vt. Four 38-inch-wide bays look out on the yard, and the end walls are two bays deep (or 6 feet 9 inches). The unit cost about $6,000 installed. Work was completed in a day and a half, except for a few finishing details. You can use the same procedure to erect a similar unit.

First, you'll need a foundation. The Dover house has a concrete slab 14 feet long and 7 feet wide, set 9 inches lower than the living-room floor. Since no interior wall divides the living room and the step-down sun room, Nova constructed a "splice" by lag-screwing 2 × 4s to the house exterior. The greenhouse rests on 2 × 6 subsills lag-screwed to the slab.

Tack the roof ridge, end-wall framing bars, and sills into place temporarily on the 2 × 4 and 2 × 6 mating surfaces, and readjust them until the dimensions of the greenhouse match the manufacturer's specifications. When all the corners are

The appealing styling, prefabricated parts, and built-in insulating qualities of sunspaces such as this can make an economical and attractive addition to most any home.

Is a Sun Room Right for Your House?

Doug Taff, president of Sunplace, Inc., says the majority of the residential glass rooms his company sells are add-ons to existing houses. But a glass room won't satisfy every home-owner's space needs, location, and budget. I asked Taff how an owner should decide if a prefabricated greenhouse is right for his house. Here's his list of the five factors you should consider:

Purpose: How do you plan to use your sunspace? Glass rooms are best suited for "outdoor-type" uses—to house a whirlpool spa or potted plants, for example. They can also be used to add living space to a kitchen or dining room, or to create a sunny family room. But think twice about using a sunspace as your guest bedroom.

Location: Where will you build the sunspace? In the northern states, the ideal location is a sunny spot where you'll get the most heat. In southern regions, you'll want a shady site. The location should also afford some privacy. And you should avoid potential hazards like falling tree branches or icicles.

Aesthetics: A glass room can add to the at-tractiveness and value of your house, but only if you choose an appropriate unit. Prefabricated sunspaces come in many styles and almost any size. Select one that will blend with your house's architecture and environment.

Cost: The average glass room costs about the same amount as a conventional room addition. You might reduce your expenses by using an existing concrete patio or carport slab as a foundation. Accessories such as ventilating fans, thermal shades, or low-emissivity glass, which allows heat in during the day but retards its escape at night, will increase cost. But you can justify purchasing these extras if they sig-nificantly reduce heating bills or increase the overall value of your house.

Dealer reputation: Nationally known sun-space manufacturers choose their dealers care-fully and usually stand behind their products. Even so, it is wise to check with several former customers before selecting a dealer. Pick one who guarantees his work, or—if you plan to install the add-on yourself—make sure the dealer agrees to provide plenty of advice and instruction.

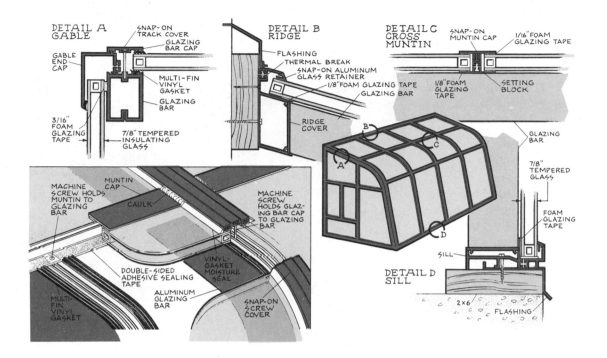

DETAIL A GABLE — SNAP-ON TRACK COVER — GLAZING BAR CAP — GABLE END CAP — MULTI-FIN VINYL GASKET — GLAZING BAR — 3/16" FOAM GLAZING TAPE — 7/8" TEMPERED INSULATING GLASS

DETAIL B RIDGE — FLASHING — THERMAL BREAK — SNAP-ON ALUMINUM GLASS RETAINER — 1/8" FOAM GLAZING TAPE — GLAZING BAR — RIDGE COVER

DETAIL C CROSS MUNTIN — SNAP-ON MUNTIN CAP — 1/16" FOAM GLAZING TAPE — 1/8" FOAM GLAZING TAPE — SETTING BLOCK — GLAZING BAR — 7/8" TEMPERED GLASS — FOAM GLAZING TAPE — SILL

DETAIL D SILL — 2×6 — FLASHING

MACHINE SCREW HOLDS MUNTIN TO GLAZING BAR — MUNTIN CAP — CAULK — MACHINE SCREW HOLDS GLAZING BAR CAP TO GLAZING BAR — DOUBLE-SIDED ADHESIVE SEALING TAPE — VINYL-GASKET MOISTURE SEAL — ALUMINUM GLAZING BAR — SNAP-ON SCREW COVER — MULTI-FIN VINYL GASKET

square, caulk the back sides of the metal beams and lag-screw them down permanently (see photos).

The glazing bars, which are the primary structural parts, go up next. They're hollow 2-by-3-inch rectangular aluminum extrusions. Like the other metal parts, the glazing bars are pre-cut, pre-painted with a baked-on enamel, and pre-drilled at the factory. To assemble them, line up the screw track running along each bar's center line with holes in the sill and ridge. Fit aluminum plugs into the hollow tops of the end-wall bars, and attach them to the bottoms of the glazing bars.

The muntins (horizontal beams) are the only remaining structural components. Cut wood spacers to the lengths specified in the installation manual, and use them to position the muntins across the glazing bars. If your sun room has windows or doors, attach the frames with screws.

Like most prefabs, the Sunplace glass room uses a "dry glazing" system. The glazing panels are two sheets of tempered 1/8-inch clear glass with a 5/8-inch hermetically sealed air space

167

1. When you're sure the subsills and attaching surfaces on the house are flat and the corners are square, caulk the back sides of the ridge, end-wall bars, and sills. Lag-screw them into place. 2. Line up the screw track running along the glazing bar's center line with pre-drilled holes in the sill and ridge.

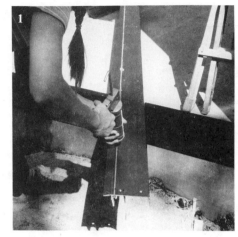

3. End-wall bars have aluminum plugs, called spigots, that attach to glazing bars. Glazing bars slip into a slot in the ridge. Later, glass slips into a similar slot above the glazing bars. 4. Screws fit through pre-drilled holes in muntins (horizontal beams) and the screw track in glazing and end-wall bars. A wood template ensures proper spacing. Muntins extend over a maximum of three bays.

5. Install the top muntin for a 40-inch sliding window. Cut 1-by-2-inch spacer templates according to the manufacturer's instructions. 6. Place multi-finned vinyl gaskets in slots in glazing bars to keep out moisture. Weep channels on either side of the screw track carry leakage or condensation into drain holes in the sill.

168

7. Apply ¹⁄₁₆-inch double-stick tape to the sill. Just before installing the glass, remove the blue backing. Place the glass panels on the tape to form a seal.

between them to improve thermal efficiency. Tempering makes the glass so tough that workers walk on the roof panels once they're installed. You can also order the panels with a bronze tint that filters out about 15 percent of the light and heat, or with a Solar Cool coating that reflects about half of the heat transmitted through clear double-paned glass.

You weatherproof the sun room with special gaskets and double-stick tape that press against the glass and keep out moisture. Check the fit of the panels before you remove the blue backing on the sealing tape. It's almost impossible to move the glass once this tape has taken hold. When the glass is in place, secure the glazing-bar caps and snap on the muntin caps. Your new glass room is ready to use.—*Text by Jack Horst, photos by the author and Ben Day, drawings by Gerhard Richter.*

28 Assembly Tips from a Pro

The Jancovics couldn't have asked for a more pastoral setting for their eastern Pennsylvania home. Their backyard slopes down to a babbling brook, and leafy oaks offer dappled shade. It's the perfect spot for a sunspace, they thought, except for one thing: Because the house sits atop a hillock a second-story sunspace was the only option. This was no problem for contractor Bob Marx of Sun Rooms of Lehigh Valley (Bath, Pa.). He built an elevated platform to hold a model 9-15-58 sunspace from Creative Structures Inc., extending the understructure 15 feet to create a second-story deck. These installation photos cover the first day's work, with tips for anyone thinking of erecting a similar kit.

(1) Erect a knee wall with temporary braces before beginning the sunspace assembly. (2) It's important to lay the sill level and square. Our pros lay a bead of caulk between the knee wall and sill before tacking it temporarily. (3) This kit from CSI comes with pre-tenoned beams that fit pre-cut mortises. As with most kits, each piece is numbered to coincide with steps in the instruction manual. Be sure to count all the pieces before you start assembly and lay them out in the order

they'll be needed. (4) Don't expect your house to be plumb or level. You might have to shim out the wall plate to make sure it's parallel with sill. (5) Before anchoring the sill make sure it is positioned correctly by checking the plumb of rear posts with a level. (6) Use a rubber mallet when setting posts to avoid damaging tenons. The mallet should also be used on all exposed surfaces to keep the redwood unscarred. (7) Have a utility knife on hand in case any of the joints are too tight and need to be shaved. (8) Use a bar clamp to draw rafters snug when attaching roof purlins and spacers. Pros toe in sheet-metal screws without pre-drilling. (9) Mahogany window units (mahogany is harder than redwood) come with the CSI kit and fit within the frame. Remove snap-in screens during assembly to avoid damage. (10) Crank window open before nailing in place. Use nails to attach windows to top framing to avoid splitting. The bottom is screwed in place. (11) Note the bridge across the door frame for extra support. It is cut flush with the opening before the door is installed. (12) It's extremely important to make a final check of square when the basic frame is complete, with rafters and front posts attached. Check with a carpenter's square and level, and measure accurately from opposite corners for identical dimensions. At this stage the sill can still be shifted

to correct any problems. If the frame is not square, the glass will not go in. (13) Apply a continuous bead of black silicone caulk around all awning windows to form a waterproof seal. When caulking roof glass, keep it neat by masking edges. (14) Nailed-on spacers provide the rabbet in which the roof glass fits. Double-stick foil-backed butyl tape is pressed into place on edges of rafters and purlins before glass is lowered into the rabbets. (15) To keep the adhesive face clean, the foil is stripped back as the glass is lowered onto the tape.

(16) Do not stand on the glass during set-in. Pros do it, but sometimes break through panes. If it's unavoidable, wear clean soft-soled shoes.

(17) Once glass is in, a tedious process of weatherproofing—caulking and sealing—follows. Don't race or skimp: It's the key to final success.

172

29 Your Choice of Sunspace Kits

Today's sunspaces come in almost any size—from a window bumpout to a two-story unit that spans the side of a house. They include greenhouses used to grow plants that can't survive outdoors, as well as sun rooms used for living space and the collecting of solar heat.

If you have the time and talent—and disposable income—you can add a sunspace to your home with one of a new generation of kits that include all the materials you'll need.

First, do you have the skills to assemble and erect the unit yourself? You can hire others to pour the foundation and do the electrical wiring, but you'll still need some carpentry experience. Most experts don't recommend erecting a sunspace without the help of a local dealer.

"Back in the old days, when sunspaces were strictly greenhouses, leaks weren't critical," says a spokesman for the National Greenhouse Manufacturers Association. But modern sun rooms may contain fine furniture. It takes a little expertise to make the sunspace leakproof.

Also, the old greenhouses used single glazing. The standard lights [panes] of glass were much easier to handle. Today the sunspace may be glazed with slabs of double glass (see next chapter, "All About Sunspace Glazing"). Even the smallest panels, 10 feet square, weigh about 50 pounds.

Do you have time to build a sunspace? Professionals can build one in a few days, but it often takes them much longer. "Allow a sufficient amount of time and expense to get the project completed," says Larry Chavez, president of Sunlite Industries, a sunspace-kit maker. And don't forget that the foundation, wiring, accessories, and finishing are "extras" that may cost as much as the kit itself.

Angled glass lets in the low winter sun. The aluminum-framed Sunspot (at right) comes with an installation video. Two people can assemble the basic 8-by-11-foot room in about 12 hours, claims the manufacturer, ODL Inc. This model, which can be ordered by your local home center or lumberyard, has a straight eave. Aluminum frames are more common than wood ones.

If you've decided to install your own sunspace, how do you choose from the many kits available? The two most important considerations are the engineering and the ease of assembly.

"Before you buy any system, be sure the manufacturer is willing and able to provide stamped engineering calculations [prepared by a registered professional engineer] verifying the integrity of the unit you propose to buy," advises William B. Gilmer, president of Regal Manufacturing, a maker of skylights and sun rooms. "The company may charge an extra $150 to $250 for the service, but it's cheap insurance," he says.

It's also essential to look carefully at the instructions beforehand. Manufacturers like The Sun Co. make your job easier by numbering parts to match step-by-step directions. But some companies sell kits that are extremely difficult for a do-it-yourselfer to assemble, warns Creative Structures, a sunspace manufacturer. You might want to look for a professionally produced installation video, one that shows you details. The company estimates that phone calls from confused buyers have dropped by three-quarters since they introduced a video. Ask to borrow or rent the video and manual, and make sure you feel confident about putting the sunspace together before you buy.

For an extra fee some companies will send a carpenter to your home to check the alignment of the sunspace's sills before you begin erecting the framing. Ask the dealer if such a service is available.

One way to assess the difficulty of building a sunspace is to check references. Get a list of satisfied customers and inspect a finished sunspace. Be skeptical of a dealer who can't give you the name of another do-it-yourselfer who has built a sunspace.

Once you've found a sunspace that's properly engineered, and you're certain you can build it with the instructions provided, you need to make some other decisions:

- Purpose and size. A room used to grow plants has different glazing and ventilation requirements than a living area. If you don't need a fancy room, you might want to look at sun porches like those made by Vegetable Factory and Solar Resources. "Not everybody can afford twelve or twenty thousand dollars for a glass structure," says Stephen R. Kenin, president of Solar Resources. His company's Solar Rooms, which sell for under $2,000, switch from solar collectors in winter to screened porches in summer.

- Foundation. Will you build it on a slab or construct a stem wall or knee wall? It's important to properly prepare the site in advance (see drawings, next page).

- Framing. Aluminum framing is almost always cheaper than wood. It usually comes in bronze, white, and mill-finished aluminum—but at least one homeowner has turned his greenhouse into a *pinkhouse*. Whatever the color, the metal should be anodized to prevent corrosion. Some aluminum structures have a baked-on enamel coating instead. If you choose one of these, make sure the coating is even, or the surface may crack and peel.

  Wood systems may be more attractive than aluminum, but they are usually more difficult to install and maintain. Laminated beams, for example, may need occasional varnishing.

Poured slabs (right) are often used when glass extends all the way to the ground.

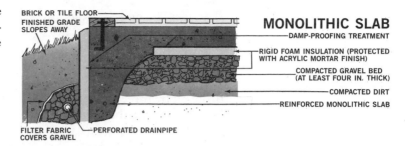

MONOLITHIC SLAB

BRICK OR TILE FLOOR
FINISHED GRADE SLOPES AWAY
DAMP-PROOFING TREATMENT
RIGID FOAM INSULATION (PROTECTED WITH ACRYLIC MORTAR FINISH)
COMPACTED GRAVEL BED (AT LEAST FOUR IN. THICK)
COMPACTED DIRT
REINFORCED MONOLITHIC SLAB
FILTER FABRIC COVERS GRAVEL
PERFORATED DRAINPIPE

Knee walls lift glass above grade. Stem walls are built like knee walls, but are shorter. Always use insulation—preferably rigid foam. To store solar heat, install a brick or tile floor atop the slab. If you grow plants, you may want a central drain.

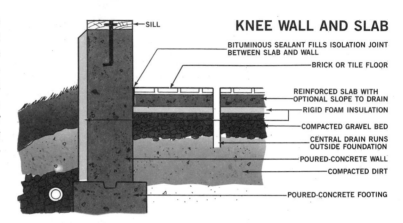

KNEE WALL AND SLAB

SILL
BITUMINOUS SEALANT FILLS ISOLATION JOINT BETWEEN SLAB AND WALL
BRICK OR TILE FLOOR
REINFORCED SLAB WITH OPTIONAL SLOPE TO DRAIN
RIGID FOAM INSULATION
COMPACTED GRAVEL BED
CENTRAL DRAIN RUNS OUTSIDE FOUNDATION
POURED-CONCRETE WALL
COMPACTED DIRT
POURED-CONCRETE FOOTING

Both aluminum- and wood-framed sunspaces can be made watertight. The sunspace should not only keep out rain and melting snow, but should also eliminate condensation that may accumulate on inside surfaces. Look for weep channels as a standard feature (see drawing on page 177). Gutters located only between the lights of glass on the upper surface of the rafters are not sufficient. What you need are gutters around all four sides of every light of glass, on the inside of the room. The gutters should overlap so that water cascades from one to the next as it travels to drainage holes.

- Style. Pick a design and roof angle that blend well with the rest of your house. Many companies offer models with a variable roof pitch, making it easier to mate the sunspace with the side of your house.
- Roofing. A clear roof admits more light, but the sunspace may overheat if you don't install shades or screens. An

Florian Greenhouse's drawing shows the assembly system for its Sierra Room sunspace. Gaskets and two-sided tape hold glass in place, but prevent glass-to-metal contact. A stainless-steel speed clip makes it easy to put the unit together, but the glazing clip that secures the glass is made of nylon, which prevents heat from traveling through the frame by metal-to-metal transfer. That's the purpose of the thermal breaks, which are also made from a nonconductive material. A rubber seal that insulates gable ends also acts as a thermal break. Like all of the better greenhouses, the Florian unit has tracks that carry away condensation. The weep channel along the sill is sloped so that water automatically drains out the weep holes.

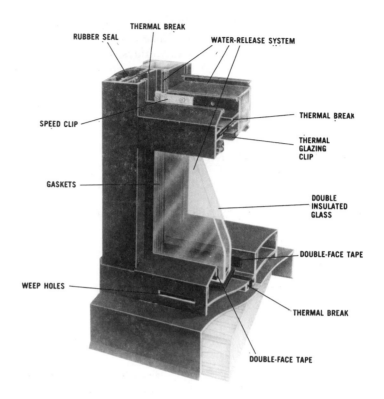

opaque roof minimizes overheating and can be insulated, but won't give you a view of the sky. Make sure the roof is engineered to support the snow and ice load you expect in winter. Check to see that the design complies with local building codes.

- Ventilation. The type of glazing and accessories you choose will determine how well you can control the temperature and humidity inside the room.
- Cost. Ask local realtors whether the addition will increase the resale price of your home. Even if it won't, the sunspace may help attract buyers. And if it's properly designed, it can benefit your home's energy budget.

The table (pages 178 and 179) lists some companies that make prefabricated sunspaces. Before you order a kit, write for more detailed information. And now there's a new kit from Four Seasons Greenhouses designed for the do-it-yourselfer.

By the time the new kit, called Mod-U-Glaze, is delivered to your home, part of the work has been done for you. While standard solarium kits are delivered in small pieces, the Mod-U-Glaze comes in preassembled modules. This should save up to two days of work time, the company claims.

The first step in building any solarium is to pour a foundation. Most homeowners prefer to have a professional do that.

SUNSPACE-KIT MANUFACTURERS

	Sizes (ft.)			Frames		Eaves		Roofs		Foundations				
No. of residential styles[1]	Height	Length	Projection	Aluminum or steel	Wood	Straight	Curved	Clear	Opaque	Slab	Stem or knee wall	Price ($)	Construction time[2]	Manufacturer
1	8′	10′5¾″–36′7⅜″	7′8¼″–11′7″	✓		✓			✓	✓		4,981–15,260	8–12 hours	Advance Energy Technologies, Solar Dr., Clifton Park NY 12065
4	6⅙′–10′	13′–any	3′–11′		✓	✓	✓	✓	✓	✓	✓	7,000–18,000	1–2 days (delivered fully assembled)	Brady & Sun 97 Webster St., Worcester MA 01603
4	7′–20′	3′–any	3′–65′		✓	✓		✓		✓	✓	40–60[4]	32 hours[5]	Classic Solar Design 3 Steuben Dr., Jericho NY 11753
5[3]	5′6¾″–7′¾″	6′7¼″–36′7¼″	3′5¼″–12′5¼″		✓	✓		✓	✓	✓	✓	2,000[6]	16–24 hours	Creative Structures 1765 Walnut Lane, Quakertown PA 18951
4	5′–27′	3′–any	1′8″–27′	✓	✓	✓	✓	✓		✓	✓	5,000[6]	2 days	Everlite Greenhouses 9315 Gerwig Lane, No. 110, Columbia MD 21046
6	5′6″–30′	5′6″–any	2′–65′	✓		✓	✓	✓		✓	✓	2,000[6]	4 days[5]	Florian Greenhouse 64 Airport Rd., West Milford NJ 07480
8[3]	5′4⅛″–20′6″	8′⅛″–32′⅜″	2′4¾″–21′5″	✓	✓	✓	✓	✓	✓	✓	✓	2,500[6]	7 days	Four Seasons Greenhouses 5005 Veterans Memorial Hwy., Holbrook NY 11741
6	8′–20′	12′6″–any	4′–17′		✓	✓		✓	✓	✓	✓	6,000–20,000	16–48 hours	Freedom Sunspace RD 5, Box 172, Freehold NJ 07728
4[3]	3′–30′	3′–any	3′–20′	✓		✓		✓		✓	✓	50–70[4]	2 days for 10′-by-20′ unit	Gammans Industries Box 1181, Newnan GA 30264
9	10′–14′	11′–24′	8′–16′		✓	✓			✓		✓	5,189–17,166	80 hours	Habitat 123 Elm St., South Deerfield MA 01373
16	4′–17′	8′–any	3′–16′	✓		✓	✓	✓		✓	✓	1,500–12,000	8–40 hours	J.A. Nearing Co. (Janco) 9390 Davis Ave., Laurel MD 20810
6	7′1″–11′	3′–any	4′1″–12′10″		✓	✓		✓	✓	✓	✓	3,000[6]	3 days	Lindal Cedar Homes 4300 S. 104th Pl., Seattle WA 98178
3	6′8 5/16″–9′9 15/16″	8′–22′	3′–11′	✓		✓	✓	✓		✓	✓	2,550–12,554	12 hours[5]	ODL Inc. 215 E. Roosevelt Ave., Zeeland MI 49464
many[3]	2′6″–30′	any	1′–30′	✓		✓		✓	✓	✓	✓	3,000[6]	6 hours[6]	Regal Manufacturing Co. Box 14578, Portland OR 97214

Then, with a Mod-U-Glaze kit, a ridge strip (included) is attached to the house, and a starter strip (also included) is attached to the foundation. These hold the modular frame sections in place (each one forms one bay). Putting in the modules is as easy as putting together a swing set, the manufacturer

SUNSPACE-KIT MANUFACTURERS

No. of residential styles[1]	Sizes (ft.)			Frames		Eaves		Roofs		Foundations		Price ($)	Construction time[2]	Manufacturer
	Height	Length	Projection	Aluminum or steel	Wood	Straight	Curved	Clear	Opaque	Slab	Stem or knee wall			
4	6'–12'	2'11⅝"–any	2'3⅛"–14'9"	✔	✔	✔	✔	✔		✔	✔	1,725–12,800	32 hours	Skytech Systems Box 763, Bloomsburg PA 17815
8[3]	8'6"–19'	8'–any	4'–25'		✔	✔			✔	✔	✔	4,800[6] (8,000–12,000 avg.)	2 days[7]	Solar Additions Box 241, Greenwich NY 12834
1	8'	12'–40'	7'	✔		✔		✔		✔	✔	1,710	2 days	Solar Resources Box 1848, Taos NM 87571
5	8'–9'4"	10'–24'	6'–10'		✔	✔		✔	✔		✔	3,300–10,000	24–36 hours	Sturdi-Built Greenhouse Manufacturing Co., 11304 S.W. Boones Ferry Rd, Portland OR 97219
many[3]	any	10'–any	4'–16'		✔	✔	✔		✔		✔	5,000[6]	2–3 days	Sun Room Co. 322 E. Main St., Leola PA 17540
4[3]	4'–16'	3'–any	3'–18'	✔	✔	✔	✔	✔		✔	✔	2,000[6]	20–40 hours	Sun Room Designs Depot & First Sts., Youngwood PA 15697
2	6'–16'7"	any	2'8"–15'4"	✔		✔	✔	✔		✔	✔	2,500–15,000	24 hours[5]	Sunbilt Solar Products by Sussman, 109-10 180th St., Jamaica NY 11433
3	7'6½"–8'1½"	7'6"–any	5'1½"–10'1½"	✔							✔	1,200–7,000	8–15 hours	Sunglo Solar Greenhouses 4441 26th Ave. W., Seattle WA 98199
4[3]	4'7"–28'	3'1"–any	1'8"–25'	✔		✔	✔				✔	1,000[6]	12 mins. per sq. ft. of glass	Sunplace, Inc. PO Box 17019, Baltimore, MD 21203
3[3]	4'6"–14'	any	1'8"–20'	✔		✔	✔			✔	✔	1,500[6] (7,500 avg.)	2 days[5]	Sunshine Rooms Box 4627, Wichita KS 67219
2[3]	7'10"–12'9"	any	6'–12'	✔	✔	✔	✔	✔			✔	1,395–50,000	1–14 days	Texas Greenhouse Co. 2524 White Settlement Rd., Fort Worth TX 76107
1	7'5¾"–10'5¾"	any	3'2¾"–15'2¾"–	✔		✔				✔	✔	35[4]	2–3 days	Vegetable Factory 71 Vanderbilt Ave., New York NY 10169

Notes: [1]Not including freestanding greenhouses or commercial units; [2]for average-size room, not including site preparation or finishing; [3]variable roof pitch on some models; [4]per square foot; [5]with two workers; [6]and up; [7]with three workers

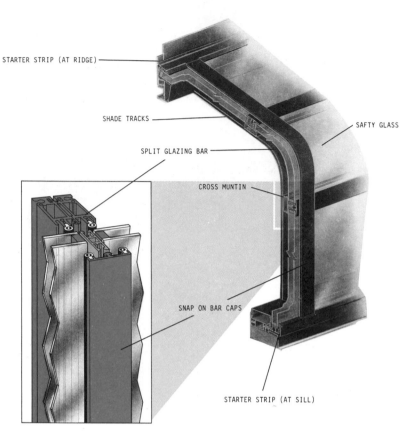

STARTER STRIP (AT RIDGE)

SHADE TRACKS

SPLIT GLAZING BAR

CROSS MUNTIN

SAFTY GLASS

SNAP ON BAR CAPS

STARTER STRIP (AT SILL)

The Mod-U-Glaze solarium kit comes in preassembled modules; each one is a bay. Glass is put in place and snap-on bar caps finish the exterior.

claims. Tempered safety-glass panels are then fitted into the frames, and outer glazing caps snap over the glass. You need a minimum of two people to assemble a solarium.

Glazing options include double-pane insulating glass and Heat Mirror, a low-emissivity glazing. Mod-U-Glaze kits are available in a variety of sizes from 3 to 15 feet in width and from 7½ feet to 10¾ feet in height. Any length in multiples of 30 inches is possible; that's the width of a bay.

Kits range from $16 to $25 per square foot of glass area, depending on size, glazing options, and company specials. Assembling the kit yourself should save about one-third on the total cost of a new solarium.

For a brochure showing types of sunspaces and giving suggestions as to siting, building permits and codes, write National Greenhouse Mfgs. Assn., P.O. Box 567, Pana, IL 62557.—*Text by Dawn Stover and Marcelle Soviero, drawings by Ed Lipinski and Mario Ferro.*

When sunspaces are used as living areas, they must be outfitted with the proper accessories. For details, see Chapter 31.

A sunspace with a cathedral ceiling made up of several skylights. For details see Chapter 32.

30 All About Sunspace Glazing

At a recent National Association of Home Builders show, I paused at the Four Seasons Solar Products booth, and Donald Staib, the company's national accounts manager, promptly beckoned me into a long sunspace flanked by a bank of heat lamps.

I passed into the first bay (glazed with double insulating glass, said the sign) and was overwhelmed by the heat. I scurried on to bay two (bronze-tinted double glass) and found an improvement to the ovenlike environment. Finally, in bay three the temperature was relatively comfortable. It was glazed with Heat Mirror, a triple sandwich with two sheets of glass and two air spaces surrounding a low-emissivity (heat reflecting) polyester film.

It was a graphic demonstration of how important the choice of glazing can be in a room that is mostly windows. And what a choice there is: not only the different glasses Four Seasons demonstrated, but several others as well. And many kinds of plastics. What glazing is best for your sunspace? That depends on climate, design and orientation of the room, and what you expect from it. Your choices also may be narrowed by your local building code—and your pocketbook. Once you understand the considerations, the data in the table can help you choose.

Glazing has a reputation as a great leaker of heat. Here's why: While an ordinary 2×4 stud wall with batt insulation has an R-value (resistance to heat flow) of about 11, a single pane of ⅛-inch glass ranks a measly R-0.89. Add a second pane of glass with a ⅝-inch air space between the panes, and it creeps up to R-2—still low enough to lose heat like mad on a cold winter night.

Much of the heat that escapes will be radiant heat— the long-wave infrared radiation emitted by everything in the room.

GLAZING CHOICES—BY THE NUMBERS

Type	U-value[1] (winter)	R-value[2] (winter)	Shading coefficient[3]	Visible light trans. (%)[4]	UV trans. (%)[5]	Cost/comments
Single glass						
Clear	1.13	0.88	1.00	90	80	Sunspaces are seldom made with single glass.
Tinted	1.13	0.88	0.85	69	43	
Reflective	1.13	0.88	0.51	27	15	
Double glass (sealed insulating glass)						
Clear	0.50	2.00	0.89	82	64	Average cost for a sunspace with clear insulating tempered glass might be $25 per sq. ft. (psf) of glazing. Tinted glass should add around $1.80 psf to that price; reflective adds around $4.70 psf.
Tinted (bronze)	0.50	2.00	0.73	63	34	
Reflective (bronze)	0.50	2.00	0.41	25	12	
Low-e glass[6]						
Clear	0.31	3.20	0.76	72	49	Low-e glass adds about $5 psf of glazing to the price of a sunspace (vs. clear insulating glass).
Tinted (bronze)	0.31	3.20	0.61	55	31	
Heat Mirror[7] (two 5/16″ spaces)						
88 (with clear glass)	0.26	3.85	0.70	71	34	Heat Mirror glazing should add about $5.90 psf of glass to the price of a sunspace (vs. clear insulating glass).
66 (with tinted glass)	0.25	4.00	0.41	42	9	
44 (with reflective glass)	0.25	4.00	0.16	12	n.a.*	
Laminated glass	1.10	0.91	0.82	79	1	Laminated glass (annealed) is about three times the price of single tempered glass.
Polycarbonate (¼″)[8]						
Clear	0.96	1.11	1.02	82	0	Polycarbonate is more costly than single tempered glass. But curved eaves of it (a typical use) may be about half the price of curved eaves of tempered glass.
Tinted (gray/bronze)	0.96	1.11	0.79	50	0	
Structured polycarbonate (8-mm)[8, 9]						
"Clear"	0.64	1.78	0.96	82	0	Structured polycarbonate costs more than single tempered glass, but much less than tempered insulating glass.
Tinted (gray/bronze)	0.64	1.78	0.61	25	0	
White	0.64	1.78	0.53	20	0	
Acrylic (⅛″)[8, 10]						
Clear	1.06	0.94	0.98	92	n.a.	Monolithic acrylics are 25–30% less than polycarbonates. Use only those appropriate for sunspace glazing.
Tinted (bronze)	1.06	0.94	0.61	27	n.a.	
Structured acrylic (16-mm)[8, 10]						
"Clear"	0.58	1.72	0.98	87	n.a.	Structured acrylic may cost more than structured polycarbonate because a heavier gauge may be required.
Tinted (bronze)	0.58	1.72	0.79	52	n.a.	
White	0.58	1.72	0.38	20	n.a.	
FRP						
Single "clear"[8]	1.14	0.87	0.98	90.5	17	Premium "clear" FRP is similar in cost to monolithic acrylic. It is used for horticultural greenhouses and hot-tub enclosures. Kalwall panels are $10–20 psf (wholesale).
Kalwall panels[11]	0.24	4.16	0.18	20	1	

Stand near a window on a cold night, and you may feel chilly, even if the air temperature is warm. That's partly because you're radiating heat to the window. Glass is nearly opaque to most infrared, so it absorbs your body heat and reradiates it, mostly outside.

Low-emissivity double glazing (see box, page 186: Talking Glazing) has a higher R-value than standard double glazing because it reflects much of the radiant heat. With a ⅝-inch air space and a low-e coating on one of the two panes the R-value generally ranges from 2.5 to 3.2, depending on the type of low-e coating. With Heat Mirror, the low-e film Four Seasons demonstrated, you can have triple-glazed windows that weigh no more than double windows, yet have an R-value of 3.8 to 4 (with two 5/16-inch air spaces).

Low-e glazing has other advantages: Its interior surface stays warmer in winter. "When it's 70 degrees [F] inside and zero outside, low-e glass will have a room-side surface temperature of 55 degrees," William Uhl Jr., residential construction marketing manager for PPG Industries told me. "Standard double glass would be 44 degrees, and single glass would be 15 degrees on the inside. With low-e glass the relative humidity in the room can be 60 percent under those conditions, and no condensate

---

Footnotes for Glazing By The Numbers:

Specifications assume ⅛-inch glass lights and ⅝-inch air spaces, unless otherwise noted. All values for tinted, reflective, and white glazing represent products commonly used in residential sunspaces, but all are available in a range of opacities. Data given for clear, tinted, reflective, laminated, and low-e glass are from PPG Ind. and represent typical production values for vertical glazing.
NOTES: [1]U-value is the heat-transfer rate through materials, measured in Btu/hr./sq. ft./deg. F temperature difference. Winter nighttime U-values are calculated assuming an outdoor temperature of 0°F, an indoor temperature of 70°, and a wind velocity of 15 mph. [2]R-value (resistance to heat flow) is the reciprocal of the U-value. [3]Shading coefficient compares the total solar heat gain through any other glazing with that through a single pane of ⅛-inch glass—which has a shading coefficient of 1. [4]Visible light transmission indicates the percentage of the visible spectrum that passes through the glazing. [5]UV (ultraviolet) transmission is given because the sun's shortwave UV energy fades fabrics. [6]Low-e glass data are for PPG's Sungate 100; other low-e products may differ. [7]Heat Mirror film comes in three types, as noted; all can be combined with different glass types. Data shown represent the common range of solar optical qualities available. [8]A range of thicknesses is used for sunspace glazing; also used for double glazing. Consult glazing or sunspace manufacturer for specifications. U- and R-values shown for single "clear" FRP are for flat sheets. For corrugated sheets, they are 1.2 and .83, respectively. [9]Sold in 6-mm–16 mm thicknesses; 8-mm is used for curved glazing. Data represent GE Plastics' Thermoclear panels. [10]Data are for Exolite panels from Cyro Ind. [11]Available in many thicknesses and opacities; data given represent 2¾-inch size. *Not available.

will form," Uhl added. The higher surface temperature of the glass also makes the room more comfortable.

Low-e glazing is a benefit in summer too. It reduces radiant heat *gain* because it reflects heat radiated from outdoor surfaces.

But a low-e glazing is more expensive than standard double glazing. Is it a good buy? All else being equal, the more extreme your climate, the better a buy it is likely to be. Andersen Corp. did a study of sunspaces in 16 cities across the country, and found that in all a properly designed sunspace could be more

TALKING GLAZING

LOW-E (EMISSIVITY) GLASS has a micron-thin layer of metal or metal oxide on one side. The coating reflects much of the infrared radiation but readily transmits visible light.

EMISSIVITY refers to the heat-emitting (radiating) propensity of a surface. The emissivity number compares a given surface with a perfect radiator, called a blackbody (emissivity, 1). Ordinary window glass has a high emissivity, meaning that it absorbs—then emits—most of the radiant heat that strikes it. With a low-e coating the glass reflects the heat instead. All else being equal, the lower the emissivity, the lower the U-value (thermal conductance—see notes below table).

HEAT MIRROR, a polyester film made by Southwall Technologies, has a low-e coating on one side. It is used as the center light in triple, or even quadruple, glazing. Glass is used for the outside lights. The additional air spaces lower the U-value of the window.

REFLECTIVE GLASS has a mirrorlike metallic coating that reflects solar energy, including visible light. It is often used on office buildings and for overhead glazing.

TINTED GLASS absorbs more solar energy than clear glass. Heat that is absorbed is radiated in all directions. Tinted and low-e glasses are often combined into high-performance windows for warm climates.

LAMINATED GLASS sandwiches a tough plastic film of polyvinyl butyral resin between two sheets of glass. If it breaks, the film holds the shards. (Laminated glass is used for car windshields.) It does not resist breakage better than ordinary glass of equal thickness, however (unless tempered glass is used).

TEMPERED GLASS has been heat-treated to increase its strength. Most sunspace manufacturers who use glass provide tempered glass because of its improved safety.

STRUCTURED PLASTIC SHEETS—made of polycarbonate or acrylic—are double-skinned assemblies with internal ribs a fraction of an inch apart. They combine structural rigidity and light weight.

KALWALL PANELS are two skins of fiberglass-reinforced plastic (FRP) with a ribbed internal structure and insulation (similar to angel hair for Christmas trees) between the skins.

energy efficient than a standard room of the same size. With low-e double insulating glass that remained true even when the sunspace faced *north*.

Heat loss is only part of the energy picture in a sunspace. You should also consider the amount of solar energy the glazing lets in. It is because of the solar gain that well-designed sunspaces can be better energy performers than conventional rooms.

But the sun also can be the enemy in sunspaces: Overheating is a common complaint. The "shading coefficient" column on the table ranks the glazings according to the amount of solar energy they admit.

In general, the colder your climate and the more heat you intend to reap from the sun, the more you need to consider a glazing with a relatively high shading coefficient.

The hotter and sunnier your climate, the more important is a lower shading coefficient. "In southern locations tinted or reflective glass is very desirable," Dr. Harold Gray, executive director of the National Greenhouse Manufacturers Association told me. "Otherwise, your sunspace can become unbearable in summer." But beware of glazings with a low shading coefficient if you want to grow light-loving plants, Gray warns. "If you just want some green plants for decoration there's very little problem. But with some flowering and fruiting plants, watch out." He advises looking for a shading coefficient above 0.70 or 0.80 if such plants are in your plans.

One popular option is to choose a lower shading coefficient for overhead glazing and a higher number for vertical glazing. Thus in summer when the sun is high in the sky (striking the overhead glazing more directly), more of it will be blocked. But in winter when the sun hangs low, more energy will pass.

The "visible light transmission" column in the table gives the percentage of sunlight in the visible spectrum each glazing transmits, and thus indicates how bright the room will be. It also suggests how well you'll see out of your sunspace when the glazing is glass or the monolithic acrylic and polycarbonate sheets. But with the structured-sheet plastics and fiberglass-reinforced plastics (FRP) that's not the whole picture. They may have good visible transmission, but the light is diffuse—great for many plants and for privacy, but not if you want a view.

Plastic is much lighter weight than glass, and it can be bent on site to form curved sections. It is also much more impact resistant. GE Plastics says its Lexan polycarbonate sheets are 250 times stronger than glass. "If you have branches overhanging the sunspace, or vandalism is a problem, a glazing that

187

resists breakage is worth considering," said Gray. "The structured-sheet plastics, especially the polycarbonates, are the most impact resistant."

Local building codes may have specific requirements for sloped or overhead glazing. If ordinary glass is used, a screen may have to be installed beneath to catch the shards if it should break. Codes generally allow laminated glass to be used without a screen, and some now permit tempered glass. Appropriate plastics are also permitted.

But plastic glazings scratch more readily than glass, they are flammable, some may yellow over time, and the monolithic sheets are flimsy, requiring closer spacing of the sunspace frame. The structured sheets don't provide a clear view. Plastics also have a high coefficient of thermal expansion, so seams are harder to seal. Special installation methods and materials must be used.

Whatever glazing you choose for your sunspace, you may find that thermal blinds and shading devices are necessary if you want it to be a comfortable living space—day and night, winter and summer—*Text by V. Elaine Gilmore.*

SOME SOURCES OF GLAZINGS MENTIONED:
The following companies make glazing and sell it to window and sunspace makers. Most do not sell glazing to consumers. Glass (including low-emissivity): AFG Ind., Box 929, Kingsport TN 37662; Ford Glass Div., Box 43343, Detroit MI 48243; Guardian Ind., 43043 W. Nine Mile Rd., Northville MI 48167; Interpane Coatings, Box 26, Deerfield WI 53531; PPG Ind., Glass Group, One PPG Place, Pittsburgh PA 15272. Heat Mirror low-e film: Southwall Technologies, 1029 Corporation Way, Palo Alto CA 94303. Acrylic and polycarbonate glazings: Cyro Ind., 100 Valley Rd., Box 950, Mount Arlington NJ 07856; GE Plastics, Structured Products Dept., One Plastics Ave., Pittsfield MA 01201; Rohm & Haas Co., Independence Mall W., Philadelphia PA 19105. FRP (fiberglass-reinforced plastic): Filon Div., 12333 S. Van Ness Ave., Box 5006, Hawthorne CA 90250; Kalwall Corp., 1111 Candia Rd., Manchester NH 03103. Laminated glass: Monsanto Co., 800 N. Lindbergh Blvd., St. Louis MO 63167 (makes butyl film used in laminated glass)

Other sources: National Greenhouse Manufacturers Assn., Box 567, Pana IL 62557; Andersen Corp., Foot N. Fifth Ave., Bayport MN 55003; Four Seasons Solar Products Corp., 5005 Veterans Memorial Hwy., Holbrook NY 11741

31 Outfitting Your Sunspace

The almost-all-glass sunspace you've just added to your house has unusual requirements that demand the right accessories, depending on where you live—how hot or cold it gets—and how you'll use the new room. But if you outfit your sunspace with the right options, it will reward you with countless hours of "outdoor living" enjoyment.

A decade ago the sun room was used primarily as a greenhouse and, through solar gain, as an auxiliary heat source. As such, the concept of thermal mass and advanced technologies like phase-change materials had been of utmost importance. Times change, however.

"We see sun rooms used primarily as living spaces today," says Volker Schmidt, an engineer for Four Seasons, a large manufacturer of sunspaces. "So things like phase-change salts are rarely used because they are bulky and difficult to modulate. Solar gain and efficiency as a heat source don't carry the importance they did a few years back."

"There are five basic things to consider when you accessorize a sun room intended as living space," says Dr. Harold Gray, director of the National Greenhouse Manufacturers Association: "overheating in summer; retention of heat, especially at night during the winter; maintaining adequate ventilation and moisture levels; providing thermal mass for some solar gain as well as a carefree floor, especially if you are planning to house a lot of plants; and providing for supplementary heat in areas with cold winters." There are many products you might buy to deal with any of these situations, but first you have to define your needs.

There are two approaches you might take to control the heat of the sun: erecting solar shades or screens either inside or outside the sunspace glazing. Solar screens are made of a spe-

See color photo on page 181.

With their wood-foam sandwich construction, the Boston Shutter & Door louvers and shutters provide an insulating performance of R-7, says the company. Exteriors are finished with white melamine laminate for summertime reflectance; interiors are finished in birch or red oak.

cially woven fiberglass or plastic mesh that the manufacturers claim blocks the sun's heat and glare with minimal interference with your view. The screens are commonly installed outside the glazing.

"By being mounted outside the sunspace glazing, solar screens cut off the sun's heat *before* it enters the room," says Mark Edwards of Phifer Wire Products.

Solar shades, on the other hand, are special translucent sun blockers, sometimes made of reflective material, that normally are mounted *inside* the glazing. (One firm, Pioneer Roll Shutter Co., makes shades that are intended exclusively for exterior use, however.) The shades are designed especially to be used in the sunspace environment, and they usually transmit ample light, but are said to block the sun's heat energy by either reflecting or filtering the infrared radiation.

Protection against the summer sun, which travels at a high angle, is generally most effective on roof glazing and the upper areas of wall glazing. As an alternative to solar shades and screens, Accent Awnings makes a retractable awning that can be attached to the main house structure and extended over the sunspace roof only when needed. This protects the solarium during the hottest parts of the day without obstructing the view.

At the opposite end of the spectrum, you may be concerned with winter thermal protection. Depending on where you live and how your sunspace is sited, you might achieve ample solar gain during winter to keep the sunspace comfortable, with enough extra energy to supplement your house's heat. Even if you do, you'll probably need supplementary heat for overcast days and night entertaining. Four Seasons' Schmidt suggests hooking up with your existing heating system as a separate zone if possible, or using a non-venting gas furnace, electric baseboards, or an air-to-air heat exchanger if excess moisture is a problem in your sunspace.

Thermal shades, made of quilted or pleated fabric—often with some kind of reflective backing—reduce heat loss through the sunspace glass. The shades generally run in a track under tension on the glazing frames to provide a tight seal and prevent sagging on curved or slanted areas. Most thermal shade systems offer a motorized option with remote control. Foam-filled shutters and louver panels like those from Boston Shutter & Door may be the best thermal protection in cold areas, but they are expensive and can be somewhat clumsy.

SOURCES:
Sunshades and screens: Castec, Inc., 7531 Coldwater Canyon Ave., North Hollywood CA 91605; Phifer Wire Products, Box 1700, Tuscaloosa AL 35403-1700; Pioneer Roll Shutter Co., 155 Glendale Ave., Sparks NV 89431; Sol-R-Veil, 635 W. 23rd St., New York NY 10011; Sun Control Products, 702 60th Ave. N.W., Rochester MN 55901; Verosol USA, Box 517, Pittsburgh PA 15230. Insulating shades and shutters: Appropriate Technology Corp., Box 975, Brattleboro VT 05301-0975; Boston Shutter & Door, Box 888, Island Mill, Keene NH 03431; Comfortex Corp., Box 728, Cohoes NY 12047; Jaksha Energy Systems, 804 Tulip Rd., Rio Rancho NM 87124. Ventilating fans: Vent-Axia, Box 2204, Woburn MA 01888; Weather Energy Systems, Box 459, West Wareham MA 02576. Flooring: American Olean Tile Co., 1000 Cannon Ave., Lansdale PA 19446; Dal-Tile Corp., Box 17130, Dallas TX 75217; Mannington Ceramic Tile, Box 1777, Lexington NC 27293; Summitville Tiles, Box 73, Summitville OH 43962.

A ventilating fan can be an important factor in keeping a sunspace from summertime overheating, but it must be weathertight and insulated for the wintertime. The TC 1000 ventilation system has an internal panel of foam insulation that is lifted up and out of the way for ventilating by a lifting motor, says Weather Energy Systems. It's then pulled down for a tight seal when the fan turns off.

Exhaust, or ventilating, fans get rid of the hot, stale air that can accumulate in sun rooms during warm weather. Supply fans are used during the winter to move the warm air of the solarium into the main house when the sunspace is used as a heat source.

Ventilating fans may be mounted high at a gable end or in the roof of a sunspace and should be insulated in some way for winter. Supply fans are mounted between the house and the sunspace, and there should be two: one mounted high to provide heated air to the house and one mounted low to provide return air from the house to the sunspace.

"For any fan system to provide a positive gain to the house, the fan aperture must be closed at night," says Paul Raymer, president of Weather Energy Systems. "Otherwise more heat will be lost at night than will be gained during the day. And if the fans are controlled automatically, as with a thermostat, it's important that any aperture-closure system also be automatic so it will work when the homeowner is not home." Both ventilating and supply fans should be thermostatically controlled.

Most sunspaces are built on a concrete slab. Not only does this provide a good foundation, it also provides thermal mass that enables you to take advantage of the sun's energy in the winter.

"If you want to make the best use of thermal mass a dark-tile or brick floor is the way to go," says Robert Kleinhans, executive director of the Tile Council of America. "Not only is such a floor good for solar gain, but it is fade proof, durable, and waterproof, and requires little maintenance—important if you will have lots of plants in the sun room or if there will be a lot of indoor-outdoor traffic."

If you plan your sunspace carefully and choose your accessories to fulfill your needs, you'll add enjoyment and value to your house with a livable all-seasons room.—*Text by Timothy Bakke.*

32 Vaulted Splice-on

W hen the owners of a Cape Cod cottage-style house decided to make an addition to their Ohio home, their primary goals were creating more living space and letting in more light. In the sun porch designed for them by architect Jack Hillbrand, they have additional room, and the light is provided in abundance by a continuous bank of double-hung windows combined with a row of low-profile bronze-tinted skylights.

Integrating the new 12-by-25-foot structure so that it appears

See color photo on page 182.

Bar top, sink, and under-counter storage in this porch addition are built under the old windows, which now serve as a pass-through. Tile floor stores solar heat.

The added porch (top) blends in admirably with the house's original lines (above).

to be part of the home's original design was accomplished by maintaining the same roof slope, shingles, and exterior siding used on the rest of the house. Inside, the south-facing porch is finished in natural yellow pine and redwood siding. The latter covers what used to be the exterior wall of the living room, as well as the unglazed portions of the new walls.

The addition incorporates a passive-solar design using a rock heat-storage zone located under the tile-faced concrete floor slab. In winter the slab absorbs and slowly radiates solar heat passing through the leafless trees above. So far, the owners haven't had to use the backup electric baseboard heaters.

In summer the porch is shaded by trees and the roof overhang running around its perimeter. When the porch, dormer, and first-floor north-side windows are opened, as well as the doors between the porch and living room, a convection loop is established that considerably reduces the need for air conditioning. Ceiling and gable fans moderate porch temperatures year-round.

194

CUTAWAY OF PORCH DORMER

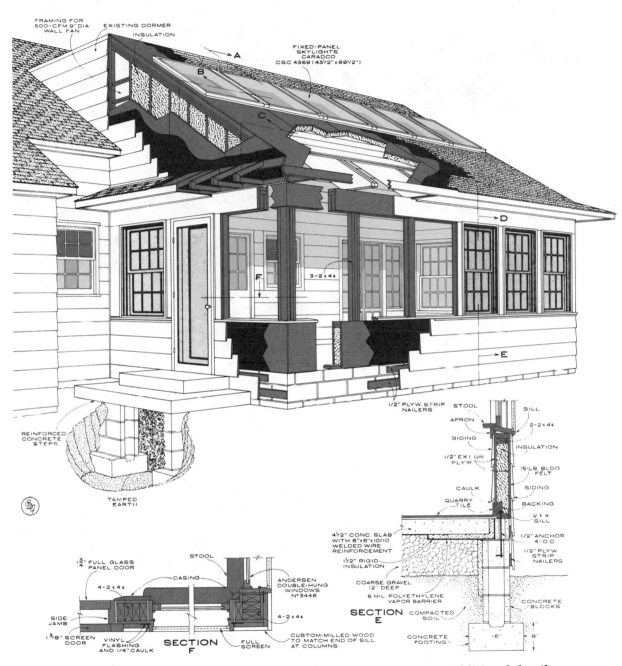

FRAMING FOR
500-CFM 9" DIA
WALL FAN

EXISTING DORMER
INSULATION

A

B

FIXED-PANEL
SKYLIGHTS
CARADCO
CSC 4369 (43½" x 69½")

C

D

3-2x4s

F

E

REINFORCED
CONCRETE
STEPS

TAMPED
EARTH

½" PLYW. STRIP
NAILERS

STOOL

APRON

SILL

2-2x4s

SIDING

INSULATION

½" EXT. GR.
PLYW.

15-LB BLDG
FELT

CAULK

SIDING

QUARRY
TILE

BACKING

2x4
SILL

4½" CONC. SLAB
WITH 6"x6"x10/10
WELDED WIRE
REINFORCEMENT

½" ANCHOR
4' O C

1½" RIGID
INSULATION

½" PLYW
STRIP
NAILERS

COARSE GRAVEL
12" DEEP

6 MIL POLYETHYLENE
VAPOR BARRIER

SECTION
E

COMPACTED
SOIL

CONCRETE
BLOCKS

CONCRETE
FOOTING

16"

8"

1¾" FULL GLASS
PANEL DOOR

STOOL

CASING

ANDERSEN
DOUBLE-HUNG
WINDOWS
N°3446

4-2x4s

SIDE
JAMB

1⅜" SCREEN
DOOR

VINYL
FLASHING
AND ¼" CAULK

SECTION
F

4-2x4s

FULL
SCREEN

CUSTOM-MILLED WOOD
TO MATCH END OF SILL
AT COLUMNS

Additional details →

195

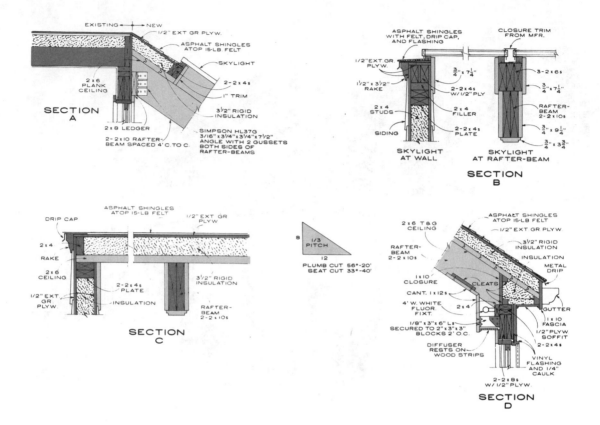

The handsome roof beams are made by spiking pairs of 2 × 10s with staggered 10d nails, then casing the assembly in ¾-inch pine (see section C in drawing). Yellow pine 2 × 10s were chosen because the lumber has a high fiber-stress rating, which allows it to carry the weight of the roofing and skylights on 4-foot centers.

Reinforced concrete steps are placed outside the porch doors. The east-facing step's apron provides terra firma for an outdoor gas grill.—*Photos by Susan Hillbrand.*

33 A Spa in the Sun

One early summer day, a Pennsylvania homeowner and his wife stepped out onto their drab concrete patio slab and began thinking about improvements in their lifestyle. Several months and much sawing and hammering later, they stepped out onto the same spot, but this time lowered themselves into a bubbling spa tub surrounded by tile and plants and sunny windows. As snow fell outside, they could hardly remember the dull slab that used to be.

Going from a useless "contractor's basic" to this kind of lux-

(continued on page 203)

A plant-filled spa room is a wonderful place for enjoying the bubbly.

SOLAR SPA ROOM

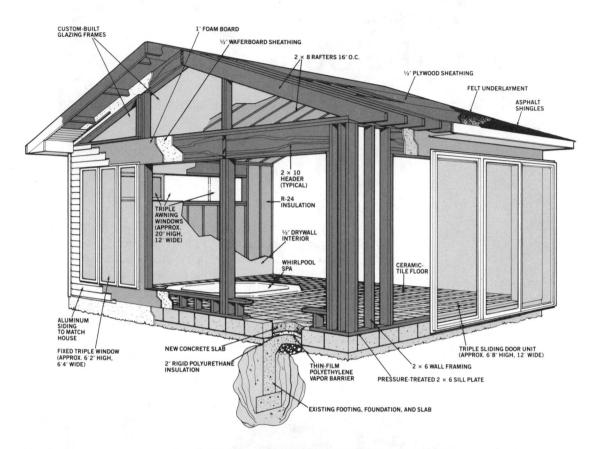

CUSTOM-BUILT
GLAZING FRAMES

1" FOAM BOARD

½" WAFERBOARD SHEATHING

2 × 8 RAFTERS 16" O.C.

½" PLYWOOD SHEATHING

FELT UNDERLAYMENT

ASPHALT
SHINGLES

2 × 10
HEADER
(TYPICAL)

R-24
INSULATION

½" DRYWALL
INTERIOR

WHIRLPOOL
SPA

CERAMIC-
TILE FLOOR

TRIPLE
AWNING
WINDOWS
(APPROX.
20" HIGH,
12' WIDE)

ALUMINUM
SIDING
TO MATCH
HOUSE

FIXED TRIPLE WINDOW
(APPROX. 6'2" HIGH,
6'4" WIDE)

NEW CONCRETE SLAB

2" RIGID POLYURETHANE
INSULATION

THIN-FILM
POLYETHYLENE
VAPOR BARRIER

TRIPLE SLIDING DOOR UNIT
(APPROX. 6'8" HIGH, 12' WIDE)

2 × 6 WALL FRAMING

PRESSURE-TREATED 2 × 6 SILL PLATE

EXISTING FOOTING, FOUNDATION, AND SLAB

Fixed windows and a sliding glass door are placed at the southern and eastern exposures to gain warmth from the winter sun, and the tiled slab (facing page) stores heat for release in the evening. Solar gain is so effective that heat can be blown into the adjacent house to cut fuel costs. Overhangs at the eaves and gables prevent summer overheating by shading the room from midday sun.

Solar design and special insulating features keep this spa room energy-efficient even when there's snow outside.

For a choice of do-it-yourself sunspace kits, see Chapter 29. This is Habitat's Solar Room with an insulated wood roof.

This screened-in sun porch features plywood shutters for yearround use. The fiberglass roof provides diffused sunlight. The porch, with its screen walls, provides the perfect setting for breezy summer dining. See details in Chapter 35.

The window panels of this glazed porch fold up for summer but provide extra insulation during the cold winters of Vermont. See details in Chapter 34.

202

The hole for the spa was cut with a concrete saw through the original patio (above). Before pouring the second layer, a wooden mold was erected around the hole. Rigid foam applied over sheathing (right) will be covered with aluminum siding.

(continued from page 197)

ury was not problem-free. The homeowners wanted the spa addition to be on the same level as the existing ground floor of their house, but the old patio slab was a step down from the house. Also, the house was cantilevered at the second floor, and the spa room would have to be tucked under this overhang with an interior soffit. Lastly, although the homeowners wanted to use the spa year-round, they didn't want it to add to their heating load.

The solution to the first problem turned out to help achieve the last requirement. To make the addition level, the homeowner decided to pour another concrete layer. First he built a concrete block wall on the original patio as a form for the new slab. Then, using a concrete saw, he chopped a hole through the existing slab to take the spa he'd bought. The old slab was covered with a plastic vapor barrier, and on top of the barrier, he placed 2 inches of rigid-foam insulation. After he'd leveled this new surface, the second concrete layer was poured. When it had set and the spa was in place, the surface was tiled. The resulting floor doubles as a heat sink that adds significantly to the passive-solar design. The ½-inch-thick earthtone tiles that cover the concrete capture heat while the sun shines on them, and hold it in the room. The tiles (from American Olean Tile, Lansdale, Pa. 19446-0271) aren't glazed, so they also provide some slip resistance. And because they're a solid color all the way through, they won't develop wear patterns.

Sun-filled spa room doubles as a casual all-season dining or entertaining area.

Though the homeowners knew passive-solar design was a good choice for their spa room, they were surprised to find that after construction was completed, their heating bills for the entire house dropped by almost 20 percent. They attribute this drop to several factors. The spa room is well insulated; according to the homeowners, the ceiling has an insulation value of R-36. This was obtained by using 2 × 12s in the construction and stuffing 11-inch fiberglass batts between them. The walls are constructed from 2 × 6 studs and filled with 6-inch fiberglass insulation. Waferboard was nailed down on the studs, providing the structural strength for the roof support, then this sheathing was covered with foil-faced inch-thick polyurethane foam. This added insulation brings the wall R-value up to 24. The walls, as well as exposed wood such as the window headers, are faced with aluminum siding for easy maintenance—and to match the existing house.

In line with this passive-solar design, fixed gable windows are framed in the southern wall. All windows—both the custom models and commercial units—are double glazed to help hold heat in the room. The western exposure has only three small, high windows for ventilation. The roof overhangs 18 inches on all three sides; the homeowners say this shades the sun room in the summer like the brim of a hat, avoiding overheating and the need for extra air conditioning. In the winter, when the sun is lower in the sky, the overhang does not impede warming rays.

Lay tile out in rented metal frame to determine best placement for trimming. Spread adhesive with flat side of trowel, then comb it with notched side of trowel; use the frame again to place tiles (right). Seat tile by striking with a wood block.

The next day, after mortar has set, spread grout diagonally; force it into joints with rubber-faced trowel. Drag a towel damp with a latex grout film remover and water solution across the surface of set tile.

"Dress" joints with damp sponge. If grout residue remains, mix softwood sawdust with water and 5% acid, using gloves. Make sure grout joints are set, then rub the mixture over the tile with a dry towel.

But perhaps one of the most important energy-saving aspects of this sun room is tucked into the interior soffit. When the sunspace temperature creeps above 75 degrees F, a thermostat-controlled fan built into the soffit switches on. Heat is carried out of the spa room through a duct running within the soffit and into the main house through a wall grille. Although the homeowners installed hot-water baseboard heating in the spa room, they rarely have to use this heat.

The spa tub itself is heavily insulated against heat loss, too. Before pouring the second concrete slab, the contractor built a wooden form around the hole chopped through the original slab. The tub, which had been factory-sprayed with urethane to prevent heat loss, was set into the hole and plumbed, then back-filled with sand. A separate gas heater outside the western wall of the sunspace heats the water for the spa, and all electrical controls are GFI-protected. The pumps and blowers for the spa are located in this same outdoor shed. For convenience, the water pipes run out to this pump house through a chase molded into the second concrete layer. According to the homeowners, this arrangement cuts down significantly on noise in the spa room. It also makes the plumbing easier to get to—no need to break up the floor when there's a leak or other problem. Also, in the interest of convenience, the underwater tub lights are not ordinary low-voltage pool bulbs. Instead, the bulbs are located in the pump house, and fiber-optic cables running through the plumbing chase bring light to special lenses in the tub. When a bulb goes out, it's easy to replace.

In the end, the homeowners have found that their versatile addition can be used for more than just water sports. Features like the ceiling fan and cathedral ceiling with exposed beams and track lighting over the spa make the room an attractive sun porch and party room. The aluminum siding was removed from the old south wall of the house, and this surface—now an interior wall—was refinished. The homeowners added a patio dining set, so their sunny spa doubles as an airy breakfast room.—*Text by Naomi Freundlich, photos courtesy American Olean.*

34 All-Seasons Sun Porch I

My Vermont retreat lacked one amenity: a spacious all-weather porch. What Alfred Lees (then the creative home-improvement editor of *Popular Science*), a young contractor named Leigh Montgomery, and I worked out together is a handsome structure that invites hospitality and relaxation.

Its flexibility of purpose—especially the overhead-storing folding window panels that transform it into a winter solarium—makes the porch adaptable to many styles of homes across the country.

A view of the sun porch with the insulating windows in the down position (left). The central entryway features an overhead door that tracks up under the roof (middle). On either side are tri-fold windows that store along the eaves (right).

ALL-WEATHER PORCH

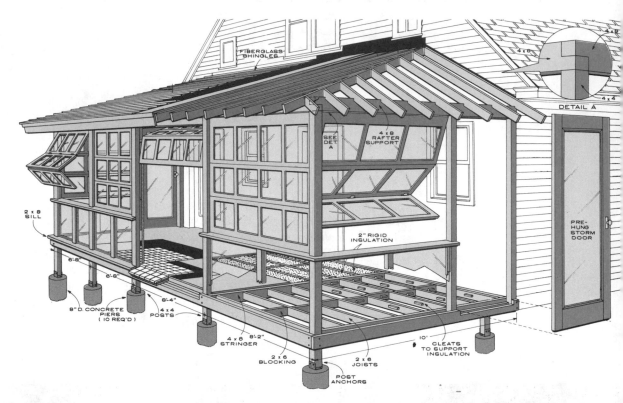

FIBERGLASS SHINGLES

4 x 8 RAFTER SUPPORT

SEE DET. A

DETAIL A

PRE-HUNG STORM DOOR

2" RIGID INSULATION

2 x 8 SILL

6'-8"

8'-8"

8'-4"

4 x 4 POSTS

8'-2"

4 x 8 STRINGER

2 x 6 BLOCKING

2 x 8 JOISTS

POST ANCHORS

10' CLEATS TO SUPPORT INSULATION

8" D. CONCRETE PIERS (10 REQ'D)

PORCH DETAILS

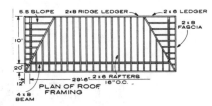

5.5 SLOPE · 2 x 8 RIDGE LEDGER · 2 x 6 LEDGER
2 x 8 FASCIA
10'
20'
12'
4 x 8 BEAM
29'-6" 2 x 8 RAFTERS 16" O.C.
PLAN OF ROOF FRAMING

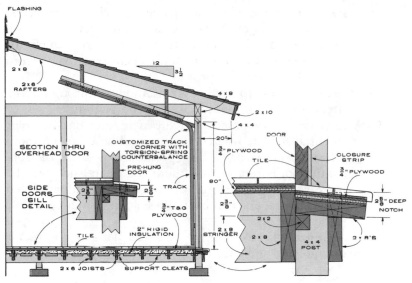

FLASHING

2 x 8

12
3½

2 x 6 RAFTERS

4 x 8

2 x 10

4 x 4

20"

SECTION THRU OVERHEAD DOOR

CUSTOMIZED TRACK CORNER WITH TORSION-SPRING COUNTERBALANCE

DOOR

¾" PLYWOOD

TILE

CLOSURE STRIP

¾" PLYWOOD

PRE-HUNG DOOR

TRACK

80"

2⅜"

2⅝" DEEP NOTCH

SIDE DOORS SILL DETAIL

2⅜"
2⅝"

2 x 2

2 x 8

2 x 8 STRINGER

TILE

¾" T&G PLYWOOD

2" RIGID INSULATION

4 x 4 POST

2 x 8'S

2 x 6 JOISTS · SUPPORT CLEATS

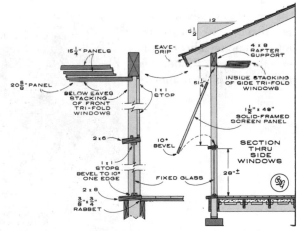

15¼" PANELS

EAVE-DRIP

12
6½

4 x 8 RAFTER SUPPORT

INSIDE STACKING OF SIDE TRI-FOLD WINDOWS

20⅝" PANEL

BELOW EAVES STACKING OF FRONT TRI-FOLD WINDOWS

1 x 1 STOP

6½"

1½" x 48" SOLID-FRAMED SCREEN PANEL

2 x 6

10° BEVEL

SECTION THRU SIDE WINDOWS

1 x 1 STOPS BEVEL TO 10° ONE EDGE

FIXED GLASS

28"±

2 x 8

¾" x ¾" RABBET

Detail (left) of color photo on page 202 shows hinged and fixed glazing panels in place for winter. Sketches above show how roof is framed and how hinged panels slide and fold against roof's underside. At center is a section showing how sill between tracks is slanted for drainage.

209

Every homeowner has individual requirements for any add-on. For this project, mine were:

- A porch—not an added room—that would retain the architectural integrity of an old farmhouse of some distinction.
- An addition that would not mask the home's view of meadows, forest, and mountains—in any season.
- A structure that could bear heavy snow loads, with a sturdy deck-support framework that wouldn't shift and crack a quarry-tile facing, even at 20 degrees below zero.
- A system of overhead-storing glazed panels that could be lowered in cool or stormy weather and would latch securely in place for the winter—plus screen panels for protection against insects (and occasional bats) from spring through early autumn.
- Three-way access to my home's main entry through doors offering the same glass-to-screen convertibility.
- A capacity for taking advantage of whatever passive-solar potential the site offered. This would have been a more pressing concern had it been possible to position the 300-square-foot porch for maximum solar exposure, but the entry wall to which the porch would have to attach faced east-southeast and was partially shaded by a huge willow at the south end.

To maximize whatever winter heat gain I'd get, contractor Leigh Montgomery and I decided to do all glazing with low-iron

The post-and-beam cage ties directly to the house but adds no weight: It rests on its own foundation piers—critical locations.

Anchor bases keep ends of posts dry, permit some alignment adjustment on piers—which are sunk below frost line.

Plywood floor sets flush with face of inner band joist. Rabbet sets sill at 10-degree slope. Beyond is center threshold.

Lay tile in thin-set mortar, right up to edge of sill; this last row of tile is positioned on sill, ready for laying.

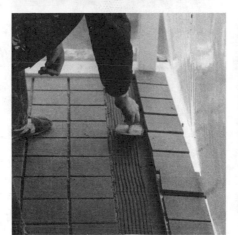

Protective wrap is lifted by builder Montgomery; he's checking space for grouting on double-bullnose recess of main-entry threshold. Ten-penny nail gives space.

Storm door comes pre-hung in steel frame you nail in rough opening.

Snug closure is ensured with adjustable channel that has vinyl sweep base.

End-wall tri-fold, next to door, mounts flush with inner faces of posts and header (note top hinges). Its bottom panel rests on railing, swings up for storage.

PARTICIPATING MANUFAC-TURERS *Lava-red quarry tile:* American Olean Tile, Lansdale PA 19446; *Three-dimensional fiberglass-based asphalt shingles:* Asphalt Roofing Mfgs. Assn., 6288 Montrose Rd., Rockville MD 20852; *Overhead door and tri-fold frames:* Fimble Door Corp., Nashua NH 03060; *Low-iron glazing, for both fixed and movable frames:* General Glass Intl. Corp., New Rochelle NY 10801; *Convertible storm doors:* J.C.Penney Co., 1301 Ave. of the Americas, New York NY 10019; *Post and rafter anchors:* Teco Products, Colliers Way, Colliers, WV 26035.

glass. Since it has few iron-oxide impurities, this glass improves solar transmission by reducing absorption within the pane; over 90 percent of the solar energy passes through to heat our floor's quarry-tile surface. Ideally this tile should be laid over an insulated concrete base, to retain solar heat (as specified for Jeff Milstein's add-on sunspace); but my potential heat gain didn't justify the installation cost. Instead, our crew insulated the underside of the plywood deck by laying rigid-foam panels in the joist cavities (see plans—leave a ½-inch air space between the foam and the plywood), then we just laid the ½-inch-thick tile in thin-set mortar.

The contractor gave the floor maximum solar exposure by using fixed panes under the railing (³⁄₁₆-inch impact-resistant thickness; standard gauge was used in all movable panels). We'd have benefited still more, of course, from double glazing, but again the expense couldn't be justified in our situation. We did complete the enclosure by installing energy-saving storm doors at each end. The glass panel snaps out to be replaced by summer screening.

In keeping with the country look of the house (the main roof

Front tri-folds swing out to store under eaves. Sharper hip-roof pitch forces end-wall tri-folds to swing in for storage, right.

Tack stop strips on inside faces of posts; you'll also need stops across sill and under rail. Mating edge is beveled to match.

Slide latch secures overhead door—up or down—by engaging slots in the track.

of which has weathered cedar shakes) we chose to roof the porch with three-dimensional fiberglass-based asphalt shingles. For a rustic accent, the thickness of the ridge tabs was doubled.

Note that my contractor chose balloon post-and-beam construction, basing each of the 10 posts on a concrete pier that's sunk below the frost line. Anchor bolts, set into each pier's top, take Teco post anchors designed not only to lift the post ends away from dampness but to permit alignment adjustment after the concrete sets. We let the piers cure several days before erecting the post-and-beam framework on them.—*Text by H.L. Kirk, photos by Leigh Montgomery and Alfred Lees.*

All-Seasons
Sun Porch II

Winter or summer, cars slow down when they pass the home of Anthony J. Wydra in the western New York town of Grand Island. The sun porch Wydra notched into the front of his house is an eye-catcher.

An eggcrate grid of redwood 2 × 4s soars out over an airy, handsomely framed structure. In summer the broad "windows" are filled with screen panels. Suspended from the projecting rafters are flower baskets and droplights for evening illumination. For winter the screens are stored and the openings are shuttered with ⅜-inch plywood. The porch still has ample illumination through glazed strip windows tucked under the eaves

See color photos on page 201.

The sun porch is shown with the plywood shutters in place for the winter.

SUN PORCH II

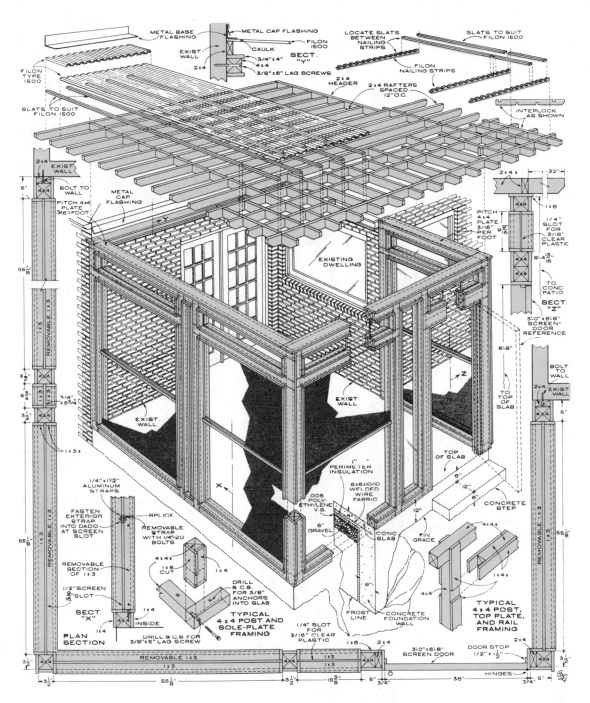

215

and through the translucent roof panels of fiberglass-reinforced plastic (FRP).

In the summer mode the porch is an ideal breezeway for breakfast and lunch (see photos, pages 200 and 201). In winter it can be used to store outdoor gear or can serve as a party room. The winter porch also doubles as an airlock entry, a buffer against chill winds when you use the house's front door.

And this is no small consideration in Grand Island, where winds can howl up to 70 mph and January can dump six feet of snow on the roof. Snow load was one of Wydra's main design concerns, and his interlocking eggcrate grid of 2 × 4s provides sturdy support for the Filon panels. (Filon is a quality brand of FRP, available in attractive "awning" stripes on a squared-off corrugation. Your Filon dealer can supply the various closure strips that are called for on the construction drawing.) Wydra decided to get Cool Rib Cinnamon in 26-by-144-inch sheets, and bought 12 of the closure strips.

Wydra's intricate design for the support structure calls for facing the 4 × 4 posts and most beams with one-by lumber. This not only added architectural detail, but permitted Wydra to erect the frame without using a single nail; the interlocking notches created by this "skinning" process make for solid joints. You can simplify construction by using redwood or pressure-treated lumber throughout, bolting members together in a conventional way.

It's all erected on a 12-foot-square concrete slab, poured without any pitch (it must be perfectly level). Wydra first dug a perimeter trench nearly a foot wide and down to frost line. After leveling six inches of gravel over the surface and erecting a perimeter form, he placed rigid insulation, as shown in the dimensioned drawing, and brought in a ready-mix truck for a continuous pour.

The FRP panels were attached to the frame with screws that have rubber gaskets under their heads (you get them where you buy Filon).

Some interior 1 × 3 facing planks are attached with screws so as to be removable. This lets you take out the screen frames and insert the shutters. Not all of the 1 × 3s must be detached, though: Just take off one side and the top and bottom so panels can be swung out or in. You only do this twice a year, and it takes less than an hour.

"One of the nicest features," Wydra says, "is that 30-inch overhang. It keeps the screens and floor dry and lets you enjoy a summer thundershower outdoors."—*Text by Alfred Lees, photos by Greg Sharko, watercolor sketch by Eugene Thompson.*

36 Two-Phase Inside-out Sun Porch

From the curb, the house seemed to match its real-estate listing: "3 BR ranch, att dbl gar, patio." But when I hopped around back, that "patio" proved to be the typical bad joke of most developments. The only access to it was the garage's back door (below, left). Inside, the home's major drawback was a cramped, dark dining room. Before putting down earnest money, the prospective home buyer asked me to propose an addition that would make the home attractive for entertaining.

Tacking a room onto the kitchen/dining wall and adding an open deck would go far in that direction—but it would also

All-too-typical back stoop from the attached garage (above) meets a useless patio slab—this one even lacks access to kitchen and dining room (windows at right in picture). First addition adds screened porch and open deck.

TWO-PHASE DECK EXTENSION

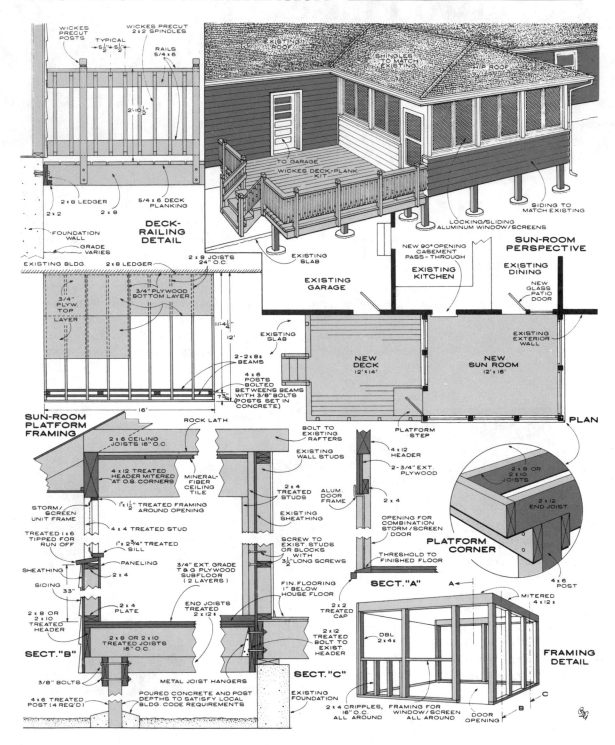

DECK-RAILING DETAIL

WICKES PRECUT POSTS
WICKES PRECUT 2x2 SPINDLES
TYPICAL 5½" + 5½"
RAILS 5/4 x 6
2'-10½"
2x8 LEDGER
5/4 x 6 DECK PLANKING
2x2
2x8
FOUNDATION WALL
GRADE VARIES

SUN-ROOM PERSPECTIVE

EXISTING ROOF
SHINGLES TO MATCH EXISTING
HIP ROOF
TO GARAGE
WICKES DECK-PLANK KIT
EXISTING SLAB
LOCKING/SLIDING ALUMINUM WINDOW/SCREENS
SIDING TO MATCH EXISTING
NEW 90° OPENING CASEMENT PASS-THROUGH

PLAN

EXISTING BLDG
2x8 LEDGER
2x8 JOISTS 24" O.C.
EXISTING SLAB
EXISTING GARAGE
EXISTING KITCHEN
EXISTING DINING
NEW GLASS PATIO DOOR
NEW DECK 12'x14'
NEW SUN ROOM 12'x16'
EXISTING EXTERIOR WALL
3/4" PLYW. TOP LAYER
3/4" PLYWOOD BOTTOM LAYER
11'-4¼'
12'
2-2x8s BEAMS
4x6 POSTS BOLTED BETWEENS BEAMS WITH 3/8" BOLTS (POSTS SET IN CONCRETE)
7¾'
7¼'
16'

SUN-ROOM PLATFORM FRAMING

ROCK LATH
2x6 CEILING JOISTS 16" O.C.
4x12 TREATED HEADER MITERED AT O.S. CORNERS
MINERAL-FIBER CEILING TILE
BOLT TO EXISTING RAFTERS
EXISTING WALL STUDS
2x4 TREATED STUDS
EXISTING SHEATHING
STORM/SCREEN UNIT FRAME
1"x1½" TREATED FRAMING AROUND OPENING
4x4 TREATED STUD
4x12 HEADER
2-3/4" EXT. PLYWOOD
2 x 4
ALUM. DOOR FRAME
OPENING FOR COMBINATION STORM/SCREEN DOOR
SCREW TO EXIST. STUDS OR BLOCKS WITH 3½" LONG SCREWS
THRESHOLD TO FINISHED FLOOR
SECT. "A"
TREATED 1x6 TIPPED FOR RUN OFF
1"x 2¾" TREATED SILL
PANELING
2x4
SHEATHING
SIDING
33"
3/4" EXT. GRADE T&G PLYWOOD SUBFLOOR (2 LAYERS)
END JOISTS TREATED 2x12s
2x8 OR 2x10 TREATED HEADER
2x4 PLATE
SECT. "B"
3/8" BOLTS
4x6 TREATED POST (4 REQ'D)
2x8 OR 2x10 TREATED JOISTS 16" O.C.
METAL JOIST HANGERS
POURED CONCRETE AND POST DEPTHS TO SATISFY LOCAL BLDG. CODE REQUIREMENTS
FIN. FLOORING 1" BELOW HOUSE FLOOR
2x2 TREATED CAP
2x12 TREATED BOLT TO EXIST. HEADER
SECT. "C"
EXISTING FOUNDATION

PLATFORM CORNER
2x8 OR 2x10 JOISTS
2x12 END JOIST
4x6 POST

FRAMING DETAIL
A
MITERED 4x12s
DBL 2x4s
B
C
2x4 CRIPPLES 16" O.C. ALL AROUND
FRAMING FOR WINDOW/SCREEN ALL AROUND
DOOR OPENING
PLATFORM STEP

The second phase of building provided an insulated sun room.

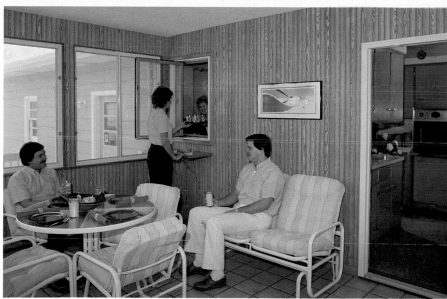

The ambitious add-ons featured in this project (Chapter 37) turned a patch of lawn (left) into a stunning entertainment area. See above and next 2 pages.

Raised deck at poolside (above) is stepped down to spacious cabana deck (1) on far side of new wing. Cantilevered roof will shade future built-in bar. Large storage area below deck railing (2) is camouflaged by a flush-fitting redwood door that hangs on a special joint.

Spacious light-filled room (left) forms the new wing. It has four eight-foot-wide glass doors—one framing the mountains to the northeast, two on the southwest wall below the skylights, and one on the fireplace wall (above). A soaring asymmetric ceiling faced with tongue-and-groove redwood emphasizes the wide-open feeling of the room. The walls, paneled with redwood siding, match the house's exterior, enhancing the illusion of being outside.

222

block two foundation windows that brought light and air to the basement. The solution? Float the addition above them, leaving access through the crawl space beneath.

The other problem was financing, so we designed the addition to be completed in two stages, as shown in the table on page 219. This spreads costs over two summers while providing instant amenities with Phase I. By carefully framing the enclosed porch to take standard window sizes, you can wrap it in screening for this coming summer, then add the glazing next year, or whenever the budget allows.

If you match the siding and roofing to the existing house, the add-on will look like part of the original design. The open deck

1. Floor joists span 2 × 12 bolted to the house and a double beam supported by posts.

2. Posts and 4 × 12 headers on a plywood platform support the roof framing.

223

3. New room is now under shelter, so the window is replaced with a patio door.

4. Three support posts are added, and the open deck is framed; header is nailed across trimmed joists.

5. For Phase II, windows replace screening.

was easy to erect, thanks to Wickes Lumber's 5/4 radius-edged, pressure-treated Deck Plank lumber, with precut components and plans. We also used the component railing system from Wickes (Box 2030, Vernon Hills, IL 60061).

For this project's first summer, we built the enclosed porch and open deck, and replaced the existing slider with a patio door for direct access from the dining room. We covered the porch floor with a frost-free ceramic tile.

The following year, the first step was to replace the screening with storm-screen window units. We then added light-colored paneling and ceiling tile and replaced the double-hung kitchen window with a casement that becomes a pass-through for serving refreshments. Since this porch is still the only source of daylight for both kitchen and dining room, we kept its furnishings bright. We might even add a skylight later. If your new sun porch happens to face south, you'll benefit from solar gain as a bonus.—*Text and photos by Mack Phillips.*

37 Indoor/Outdoor Deck and Sun Room

My wife, Rita, and I spend as much time outside as inside our house. But despite a swimming pool and a large piece of property, our backyard was not really set up for outdoor living.

A small raised deck, our main outdoor dining area, was cramped with four people on it. Steep, narrow stairs made a lower-level deck practically useless for entertaining (see photo below). Railroad ties, dug into a steep slope, led up to the pool. Some visitors found the climb difficult—and poolside entertaining was inconvenient.

See color photos on pages 220—222.

The shallow depth of the pass-through window creates a deep sill that's handy for food placement. The oil-tank fill pipe is hidden under a removable deck section and is framed by beams and joists (right).

A duckboard for the summer hose is tucked in a niche between the upper and lower decks. At right, door to second under-deck storage space pulls up and out. The top of a 1×4, ripped in half at a 45 degree angle, forms the door's top rail; it hooks over the mating piece mounted to the deck joist above the compartment.

An electronic bug killer mounted on the nearby work shed lures insects away from the grill, shown on the main deck by the resided garage.

INDOOR/OUTDOOR EXTENSION PLAN

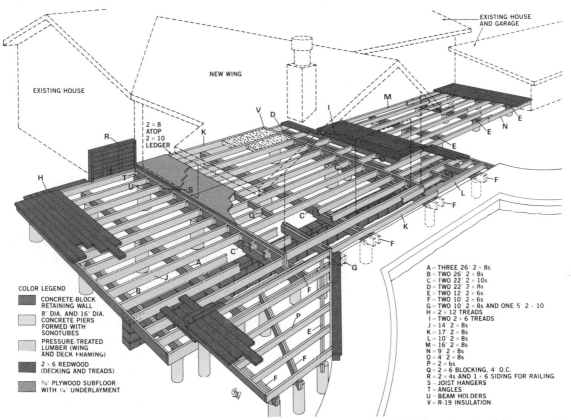

EXISTING HOUSE AND GARAGE

NEW WING

EXISTING HOUSE

2 × 8 ATOP 2 × 10 LEDGER

COLOR LEGEND

- CONCRETE-BLOCK RETAINING WALL
- 8" DIA. AND 16" DIA. CONCRETE PIERS FORMED WITH SONOTUBES
- PRESSURE-TREATED LUMBER (WING AND DECK FRAMING)
- 2 × 6 REDWOOD (DECKING AND TREADS)
- ¾" PLYWOOD SUBFLOOR WITH ¼" UNDERLAYMENT

A = THREE 26' 2 × 8s
B = TWO 26' 2 × 8s
C = TWO 22' 2 × 10s
D = TWO 22' 2 × 8s
E = TWO 12' 2 × 6s
F = TWO 10' 2 × 6s
G = TWO 10' 2 × 8s AND ONE 5' 2 × 10
H = 2 × 12 TREADS
I = TWO 2 × 6 TREADS
J = 14' 2 × 8s
K = 17' 2 × 8s
L = 10' 2 × 8s
M = 16' 2 × 8s
N = 9' 2 × 8s
O = 4' 2 × 8s
P = 2 × 6s
Q = 2 × 6 BLOCKING, 4' O.C.
R = 2 × 4s AND 1 × 6 SIDING FOR RAILING
S = JOIST HANGERS
T = ANGLES
U = BEAM HOLDERS
V = R-19 INSULATION

Both wing and deck foundations (1) rest on concrete piers topped with galvanized Teco post bases (2). Beveled wood spacers adapt the fasteners to fit the double beams (see diagram, above), which are attached with galvanized nails. Galvanized joist hangers (3) anchor the joists to the end beams; where the joists *cross* a beam, they're toenailed in place (use only galvanized fasteners). Stringers for the stairs (4) are notched over the deck frame.

1   2   3   4

To unify the house and pool area, we decided to build an indoor/outdoor room encircled by easy-access decks (see "after" photo, pages 220 to 222). In the process we developed design and construction tricks adaptable to many outdoor-living projects. They include:

- A concrete-pier foundation.
- A knee-wall building support.
- Multi-level decking.
- Low-rise steps.
- Under-deck storage.
- A kitchen pass-through.

The first step was planning. After discussing how we want to use our property, we decided to replace the old raised deck with a new wing to bridge the dip between house and pool. We also built a large deck linking house and garage. This serves as the main outdoor dining area and the entry to the multi-level deck complex.

A set of L-shaped steps lead from the ground-level deck to the new wing and a wraparound deck facing the pool. For easy climbing, the stairs have low risers and broad treads.

At the far side of the pool a raised trapezoid-shaped deck allows sunning away from the crowd. The sun deck is stepped down to a secluded cabana deck on the far side of the new room.

We wanted to avoid extensive excavation, and we wanted a structural link between the new wing and decking. So we built a concrete-pier foundation using Sonotubes, the cylindrical cardboard forms that are usually sunk in the ground for concrete footings.

The building method was simple. Using a backhoe and post-hole digger, we dug holes below the frost line and inserted the forms. After pouring in a layer of stones for drainage, we filled the forms with concrete (using a wheelbarrow and ramp as needed) and inserted anchor bolts. When the concrete cured, we attached U-shaped fasteners to hold the beams that support both deck and wing subframing.

Framing for the new wing rests on only six concrete piers. For extra stability, the wing sits atop a concrete block retaining wall, which extends the width of the upper decking (see drawing). This 3-foot-high knee wall provides firm anchorage for both room and decking, with far less work than that required for a conventional foundation. The wall also greatly simplified framing of both deck and wing because all beams are installed on the same level. (Note in the framing sketch that the floor joists for the enclosed room sit 1½ inches higher than the deck joists. Decking planks are 1½ inches thick.)

Building the stairs was simple once we determined the dimensions of treads (two 2 × 6s) and risers (6 inches). Using two boards for each tread aids drainage while visually blending the stairs with the decking.

To store equipment and outdoor furniture, I designed two under-deck storage areas and a pull-up hatch for the oil-tank fill pipe (see photos, previous page). To wed the redwood add-ons to the existing house, we re-sided it and installed new windows, including a sliding window for passing food from kitchen to deck. The window is shorter and shallower than the old double-hung one, so we had to reframe the opening.

Once the decking was laid and all outdoor finish work was done, we began work on the passive-solar all-season room.

This spacious, airy all-seasons room is the centerpiece of our renovation. Encircled by multi-level decking, the room links the house with the landscaped pool area. In summer the room serves as a low-maintenance passageway for dripping guests and as an inviting refuge from the rain. In winter the new wing becomes a cozy retreat.

Our design strategies apply to anyone who wants to add an outdoor-oriented room. They include:

- Planning skylight placement for winter solar gain.
- Building an open, Belgian truss-roof system with an exposed-beam cathedral ceiling.
- Using oversize sliding glass doors to provide an immediate visual link with the outdoors.
- Facing inner walls with rough-sawn redwood siding.
- Installing a low-maintenance vinyl-tile floor.
- Installing security wiring during construction.

For maximum solar gain in winter, we designed four skylights into the southwest-facing roof. A large tree shades the skylights in summer, so we don't need the more-costly venting types; a ceiling fan works fine. In winter the asymmetric roof encourages snow dumping, an important concern for this site in New York state.

We designed the asymmetric roof for architectural distinction as well as solar practicality. But the dual-pitch roof made careful construction even more critical. For adequate strength, we chose a Belgian open-truss design with two sets of collar

WING ADDITION

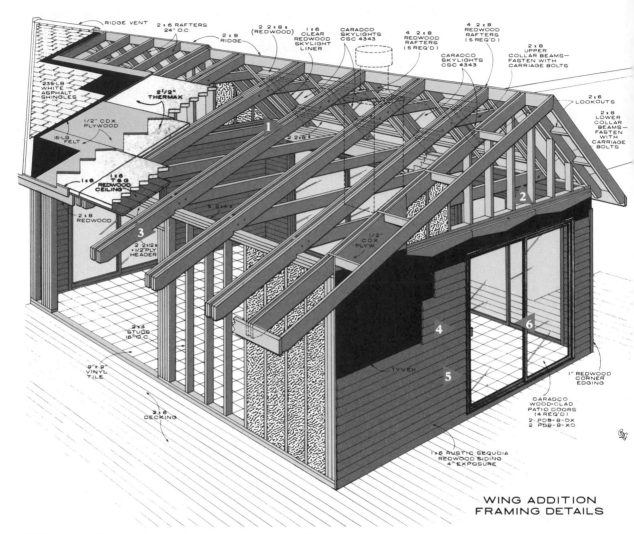

RIDGE VENT

2 x 6 RAFTERS
24" O.C.

2 x 8
RIDGE

2 2 x 8's
(REDWOOD)

1 x 6
CLEAR
REDWOOD
SKYLIGHT
LINER

CARADCO
SKYLIGHTS
CSC 4343

4 2 x 8
REDWOOD
RAFTERS
(5 REQ'D)

4 2 x 8
REDWOOD
RAFTERS
(5 REQ'D)

2 x 8
UPPER
COLLAR BEAMS—
FASTEN WITH
CARRIAGE BOLTS

2 x 6
LOOKOUTS

235-LB
WHITE
ASPHALT
SHINGLES

2 1/2"
THERMAX

CARADCO
SKYLIGHTS
CSC 4343

2 x 8
LOWER
COLLAR
BEAMS—
FASTEN
WITH
CARRIAGE
BOLTS

1/2" CDX
PLYWOOD

15-LB
FELT

2 2 x 8's

1 x 6
T&G
REDWOOD
CEILING

1 x 6

2 x 8
REDWOOD

3 2 x 4's

1/2"
CDX
PLYW.

2 2 x12's
+ 1/2" PLY.
HEADER

2 x 4
STUDS
16" O.C.

9" x 9"
VINYL
TILE

TYVEK

1" REDWOOD
CORNER
EDGING

2 x 8
DECKING

CARADCO
WOOD-CLAD
PATIO DOORS
(4 REQ'D)
2 - PDB-8-OX
2 - PDB-8-XO

1 x 8 RUSTIC SEQUOIA
REDWOOD SIDING
4" EXPOSURE

**WING ADDITION
FRAMING DETAILS**

Pointer numbers refer to photo sequence on facing page.

230

Massive double rafters sandwich collar beams, forming a rugged roof truss that creates built-in frame for skylights (1) with ultraviolet-resistant double-pane tempered glass. Ceiling fan provides air movement for ventilation. Track lights atop collar beams (2) swivel 360 degrees for dramatic lighting effects not possible with concealed lighting.

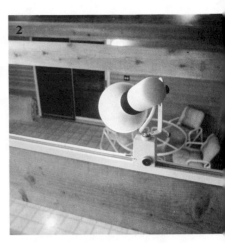

Programmable security system (3) inside main house remotely controls seven pole-mounted outdoor spotlights. Lights, divided into three zones, can also be controlled by switches in new wing (4). (For safety around swimming pool, even indoor electric circuits are protected by ground-fault interrupters.)

Pop-out security switch in a door frame (5) triggers alarm when door is opened. Switch can be wired to any type of alarm—author chose siren. Sturdy plunger-type lock on Caradco glass doors (6) allows doors to remain slightly open for ventilation.

beams sandwiched between massive four-beam rafters (see drawing).

Doubling up on either side of the collar beams disperses the roof load (which would normally require supports 16 inches on center) while creating the soaring cathedral ceiling. For roof strength as well as good looks, we bridged the trusses with a redwood tongue-and-groove ceiling. Thermax rigid-board insulation topped by plywood decking, building paper, and asphalt shingles complete the roof. To prevent rot in the dead-air space where the new wing ties into the old roof, we installed a 10-foot length of ridge vent.

The truss roof allowed us to conceal a track-lighting system atop the collar beams instead of mounting the tracks on ceiling or walls. We ran the wiring directly down into the wall. The effect is elegant—the light appears to be floating up on top.

We planned the truss to create a built-in frame for the 4-foot-square double-pane Caradco skylights, saving one step in installation. But the unconventional roofing system made it impractical to install the windows from inside. To ease placement from the outside, we nailed temporary pegs of wood to the top corners of the opening. These pegs projected no more than 1½ inches from the opening, just enough to hook the skylight frame (without touching the glass) as we lifted the window into position.

The dramatic high ceiling punctuated by light streaming in from the skylights is just part of the open, airy look so essential to our design. To give the room more of the outdoor feeling we craved, we installed four oversize 8-foot-wide sliding glass doors with a total of 20 percent more glass than standard 6-foot doors. The door frames came unassembled, but Caradco supplied a detailed 25-step installation booklet, which we followed with no trouble.

After we mounted the doors, we wired a security-alarm button into the frame. (We also installed a computer-controlled security-lighting system—see captions for details.)

To enhance the outdoor illusion, we finished the walls with the same rustic sequoia siding used on the outside. The unfinished rough-sawn texture visually links indoors with out—and requires no maintenance.

Before we put up the outside siding, we wrapped the house with Tyvek, an air-infiltration barrier made of spun-bonded olefin. Neither film nor paper, this sheet of high-density polyethylene fiber keeps cold air from penetrating seams and cracks while allowing free moisture flow, preventing condensation problems.

Finally, we installed a rugged, low-maintenance Armstrong vinyl-tile floor. Because the wing is built over soil, we used ¾-inch pressure-treated plywood as an underlayment with ¼-inch Luan plywood on top. After snapping intersecting chalk lines and dry-laying the tiles for fit, we applied mastic to a quarter of the room at a time, then laid the tiles alternately along the two chalk lines.

We also installed a one-piece heat-circulating fireplace to make the room as inviting on cold winter nights as it is by day.

IDEAS YOU CAN BUILD INTO A FIREPLACE

When I picked up my sketchbook to plan a fireplace wall, I aimed for architectural drama—and structural efficiency. The zero-clearance fireplace I'd ordered for my new wing required no extra floor supports, only a noncombustible hearth, according to the manufacturer (Heatilator, 1915 W. Saunders Rd., Mount Pleasant, Iowa 52641).

But I had more in mind: a stunning ceramic-tile mural. I wanted a vertical sweep of color that would lift your eyes to the roof peak. And I wanted a raised tiled hearth that would double as a seat. But I was concerned that a platform hearth might not withstand the inevitable settling.

I also wanted outside-air intakes for efficient combustion. But the fireplace is on the end wall. I didn't want those louvered vents right by the pool, and I fretted that I'd have no way to check the system once the surround wall was closed.

The solutions to these problems are visible in the drawing at right. They include:
- Bands of ever-lighter ascending colors in the tile facing, from brown through red to orange.
- A ruggedly framed cross-braced platform hearth.
- Outside-air intakes ducted through the floor.
- Removable wall panels for air-vent access.

The installation went smoothly. First, I framed the platform hearth that doubles as a fireplace support. I tied it into a ledger on the back wall and added an extra joist under the floor, at the center, which rests on a block wall at one end and its own concrete pier at the other. Everything ties together, so the

The stunning facade of this fireplace cleverly conceals air intakes, storage areas, and a useful platform hearth.

weight is distributed throughout the entire structure—there won't be any sag.

After framing the hearth and installing its plywood floor, I got two helpers to lift the fireplace into position. I then installed Heatilator's outside-air kit as directed, except that I drilled holes for the duct through both the platform and floor (see drawing).

234

IDEAS YOU CAN BUILD INTO A FIREPLACE

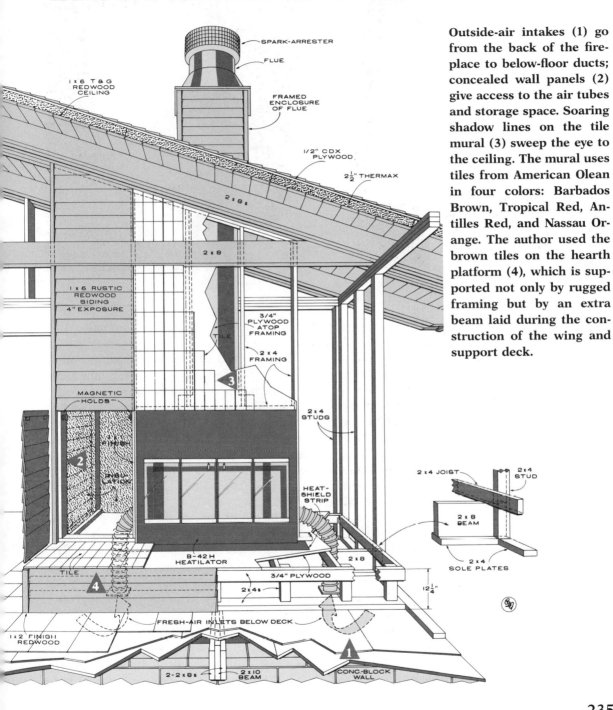

SPARK-ARRESTER

FLUE

FRAMED
ENCLOSURE
OF FLUE

1 x 6 T & G
REDWOOD
CEILING

1/2" CDX
PLYWOOD

2½" THERMAX

2 x 8s

2 x 8

1 x 6 RUSTIC
REDWOOD
SIDING
4" EXPOSURE

3/4"
PLYWOOD
ATOP
FRAMING

TILE

2 x 4
FRAMING

MAGNETIC
HOLDS

2 x 4
STUDS

FINISH

INSULATION

HEAT-
SHIELD
STRIP

B-42H
HEATILATOR

2 x 8

2 x 4 JOIST

2 x 4
STUD

2 x 8
BEAM

2 x 4
SOLE PLATES

TILE

3/4" PLYWOOD

2 x 4s

12¼"

1 x 2 FINISH
REDWOOD

FRESH-AIR INLETS BELOW DECK

2-2 x 8s

2 x 10
BEAM

CONC-BLOCK
WALL

Outside-air intakes (1) go from the back of the fireplace to below-floor ducts; concealed wall panels (2) give access to the air tubes and storage space. Soaring shadow lines on the tile mural (3) sweep the eye to the ceiling. The mural uses tiles from American Olean in four colors: Barbados Brown, Tropical Red, Antilles Red, and Nassau Orange. The author used the brown tiles on the hearth platform (4), which is supported not only by rugged framing but by an extra beam laid during the construction of the wing and support deck.

It was uncomfortable lying on my back under the house, but this way the ducts don't show.

Next, I put together the sections of Heatilator's double-walled air-cooled chimney, figuring out from my roof pitch how high to go for a proper draft. The height also conforms to local code.

Finally, I erected the studding for the surround wall, leaving two cavities on the front (see drawing). I closed the holes with panels made of the same redwood siding used on the rest of the wall, and used magnetic touch latches for a seamless-seeming fit. The access panels let me come in behind the fireplace to check on the air kit and flue. The panels also give me hidden storage for valuables.

I fastened plywood to the studding over the fireplace to serve as a base for the tile. For the mural, I chose 3-by-6-inch Caribbean II tile from American Olean (Lansdale, Pa. 19446-0271), partly because all the vibrant colors were available with a glazed, rounded "bullnose" edge on either a long or short side. This let me use butting bullnose edges to attain a vertical grooving effect in the mural and get finished edges on my hearth. I wanted to create a design using the shape as well as the color of the tile.

The mural was planned to minimize cutting, though it jumps a wall beam. Measuring for the triangle above the beam was critical. I marked the cut lines on each tile, then took them to a retail tile shop for cutting. I installed the hearth tiles in a conventional manner with a latex mortar bed. But I realized in the middle of the job that I couldn't put the wall tiles up the same way: It's too messy a job and the tiles would fall off since the mortar takes 24 hours to set up.

So I used Scotch-Grip industrial adhesive, made by 3M Co., putting five little dabs on each tile and placing it on the wall, holding for a second or so. It has great grab and sticks to the wall right away. But I had 15 minutes before it finally set, so I could wiggle the tile a bit if it needed alignment. To finish the job, I applied a brown grout on both hearth and wall tiles.—*Text by W. David Houser, photos by Greg Sharko and Rita Houser, drawings by Eugene Thompson and Carl De Groote.*

38 Self-sufficient Sun Room

The owners of this Illinois home knew they wanted more space for entertaining and relaxing. They also knew they weren't willing to put up with higher heating bills to keep a new addition warm during winter.

The solution? Unlike the "Vaulted Splice-on" featured earlier in this book (a two-story addition grafted onto a specific house design), the passive sun room they've come up with could replace a south-facing porch on virtually any home. It boasts a quarry tile floor that absorbs and radiates warmth from sunlight streaming through sliding glass doors facing south and east. The mini-blinds behind the glazing are fully raised on sunny winter days but closed at night to conserve the warmth

See color photo page 239.

The old screened porch above was replaced with the expanded structure at right.

238

The tiled interior of the renovated porch. Because it is well insulated, the space doesn't result in added heating costs.

This half-octagon sunspace offers wraparound view of the garden. Low-voltage lighting makes the view appealing by night, as well. See details in Chapter 39.

SELF-SUFFICIENT SUN ROOM

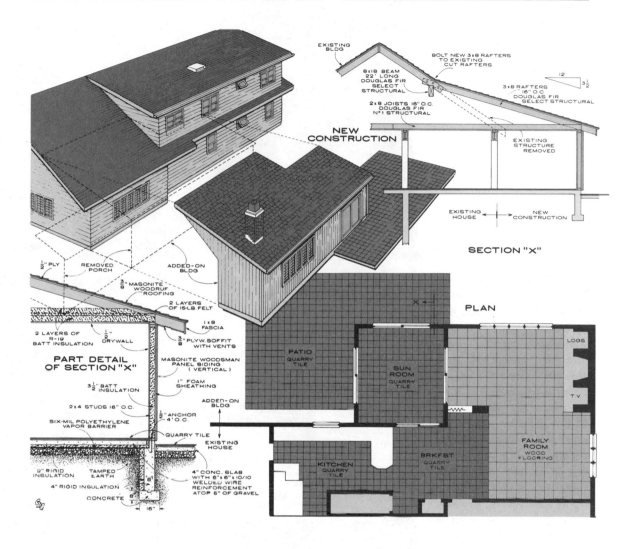

EXISTING BLDG

BOLT NEW 3x8 RAFTERS TO EXISTING CUT RAFTERS

8x18 BEAM 22' LONG DOUGLAS FIR SELECT STRUCTURAL

3x8 RAFTERS 16" O.C. DOUGLAS FIR SELECT STRUCTURAL

2x8 JOISTS 16" O.C. DOUGLAS FIR N°1 STRUCTURAL

NEW CONSTRUCTION

EXISTING STRUCTURE REMOVED

EXISTING HOUSE   NEW CONSTRUCTION

SECTION "X"

REMOVED PORCH

ADDED-ON BLDG

$\frac{1}{2}$" PLY

$\frac{3}{8}$" MASONITE WOODRUF ROOFING

2 LAYERS OF 15-LB. FELT

1 x 6 FASCIA

2 LAYERS OF R-19 BATT INSULATION

$\frac{1}{2}$" DRYWALL

$\frac{3}{8}$" PLYW. SOFFIT WITH VENTS

MASONITE WOODSMAN PANEL SIDING (VERTICAL)

PART DETAIL OF SECTION "X"

$3\frac{1}{2}$" BATT INSULATION

1" FOAM SHEATHING

2x4 STUDS 16" O.C.

ADDED-ON BLDG

SIX-MIL POLYETHYLENE VAPOR BARRIER

$\frac{1}{2}$" ANCHOR 4' O.C.

QUARRY TILE

EXISTING HOUSE

2" RIGID INSULATION

TAMPED EARTH

4" CONC. SLAB WITH 6"x 6" x 10/10 WELDED WIRE REINFORCEMENT ATOP 5" OF GRAVEL

4" RIGID INSULATION

CONCRETE

PLAN

LOGS

T.V.

PATIO QUARRY TILE

SUN ROOM QUARRY TILE

FAMILY ROOM WOOD FLOORING

KITCHEN QUARRY TILE

BRKFST QUARRY TILE

soaked up by the dark masonry flooring (Lava Red quarry tile, available at Color Tile outlets). On such days, the sun room remains comfortable well into the evening, without any backup heat. Beyond this self-sufficient corner, extra space was added to an existing family room by knocking out most of a wall. The house's existing heating system was adequate to keep the expanded room cozy when the sliding door between it and the

Walls are framed flat on the slab, and insulating sheathing is nailed in place (1). Walls are raised and propped vertically while corners are joined (2).

Masonite's wood-fiber shingles were used to roof both the sun-room addition and the existing house (3). The patio slab is stepped down from the sun-room slab. Tiles are set in rows on the adhesive-coated slab, leaving space for grout lines (4). Cut the tiles with a tile cutter to fit along walls by scoring the tile and snapping it in half. When applying grout, work it thoroughly into joints. Remove excess grout first with a wet sponge and later with a dry abrasive cleaning pad. The same tiling technique was used on the outdoor slab. A 3-inch step-down and slight pitch prevents puddling or freezing against the glass-door sills.

sun room is kept closed. (Note that on the floor plan, all four walls of the sun room have a sliding glass door.)

The homeowners began by dismantling the old screened porch shown in the "before" photo. The material was left at the site so lumber could be salvaged to reduce costs.

A trench for footings and foundation was dug beyond the perimeter of the existing porch slab. Because the sun room was to be independent of the home's heating and air conditioning, that part of the extension was insulated with rigid foam, as shown in the section below. The sun-room slab was poured over 2 inches of foam so that the heat it absorbed wouldn't be lost to the earth beneath. Once the forms were removed from the extension floor slab, a stepped-down patio slab was poured, with simpler footings pitched slightly away from the house for drainage.

After the walls were raised, a new roof was added—spliced into the cutaway existing roof—with both new and cutaway rafters butting against an added support beam. The roof over the sun-room section ties into the house's second story, with the rafters notched over a ledger lag-screwed into existing studs. For efficient solar heating, the homeowners dropped the ceiling of the sun-room area and packed the space above with insulation. Over the adjacent family room, the drywall ceiling was nailed directly to the bottom of the new rafters for a cathedral effect. (R-19 fiberglass batts were stapled between the rafters first, however.)

Masonite wood-fiber shingles were chosen for the roofing, and because these 12-by-48-inch strips nail up quickly, it was no chore to re-shingle the existing roof to match. To complete the exterior, a Masonite textured panel siding was applied to the walls. Besides complementing the appearance of the roof, the high-density siding material adds somewhat to the insulation rating of the walls.

Energy efficiency was of prime importance in the selection of materials for the sun room's interior. The walls were insulated with 3½-inch batts, which were then covered with a vapor barrier of 6-mil polyethylene stapled across the studs. The quarry tiles are thermally coupled to the heat-storing masonry mass beneath.

Installation of the ½-inch-thick tiles is simple; all the tools necessary are available from tile specialty outlets. After grouting, coat the surface with silicone sealer to prevent dirt and moisture penetration.—*Text by Alfred Lees.*

39 Add-on Garden Bar/Sun Room

S ome great home improvements grow from modest intentions. This lovely addition began as a simple wish—by homeowners Robert and Karen Benz—for a sheltered area for outdoor dining. They'd inherited a barren concrete patio outside the kitchen of their Wisconsin house, and their first thought was to erect a lightweight frame to create a screened room large enough for a dining table.

But when they consulted architect Bill Winters of Milwaukee's Junge & Associates, they realized that such a shelter would only be usable for—at most—four months of their climate's year. So the screened room evolved into a fully winterized addition that's not only comfortable year-round, but complements the existing architecture far better than a screened room would have.

New concrete was poured atop and beyond the existing patio, resulting in an 8-inch slab on grade. When the new pour had cured, plywood underlayment was nailed over 1 × 2 sleepers, and the walls were framed to create a giant window bay.

Two box beams project from the original exterior wall of the house to rest on the full-height brick wall behind the fireplace. The section detail, below right, shows how these beams are clad to create a top trough into which fluorescent fixtures fit to provide indirect lighting bounced off the faceted cathedral ceiling above. As the color overlay on the floor plan indicates, the roof framing is somewhat complex, especially where it ties into the existing structure. Specifics differ with each situation; so unless you're comfortable with opening the main roof deck to pass new framing members through for nailing to existing rafters, it's best to call on the services of a professional builder to engineer the roof supports. You could then take over to apply the ply-

See color photo on page 240.

The sun room measures roughly 17 by 22 feet and is sided with vertical 1 × 10 rough-sawn cedar. All windows are operable casements for ventilation, and there are skylights on both sides of the main ridge. Inside, a built-in wet bar and freestanding fireplace offer hospitality; the room is furnished for entertaining. Folding doors hide bar when it's not in use. Brick wall and hearth are flanked by walls of windows.

wood deck and the asphalt shingles. Shingling is a labor-intensive chore on a faceted roof such as this, with much angle trimming. This makes it a practical, money-saving do-it-yourself job.

The only hint that those angled fascia boards conceal the gutter system is the downspout at the far left in the exterior photo. The runoff can be diverted to catch basins for watering the garden during dry spells.

GARDEN BAR/SUN ROOM

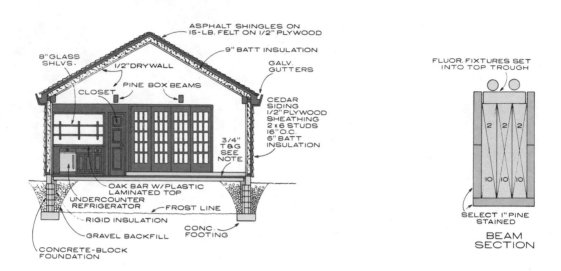

ASPHALT SHINGLES ON
15-LB. FELT ON 1/2" PLYWOOD

9" BATT INSULATION

8" GLASS SHLVS.

1/2" DRYWALL

GALV. GUTTERS

CLOSET

PINE BOX BEAMS

CEDAR SIDING
1/2" PLYWOOD SHEATHING
2 x 6 STUDS
16" O.C.
6" BATT INSULATION

3/4" T&G SEE NOTE

OAK BAR W/PLASTIC LAMINATED TOP

UNDERCOUNTER REFRIGERATOR

FROST LINE

RIGID INSULATION

GRAVEL BACKFILL

CONC. FOOTING

CONCRETE-BLOCK FOUNDATION

FLUOR. FIXTURES SET INTO TOP TROUGH

2 2 2

10 10 10

SELECT 1" PINE STAINED

BEAM SECTION

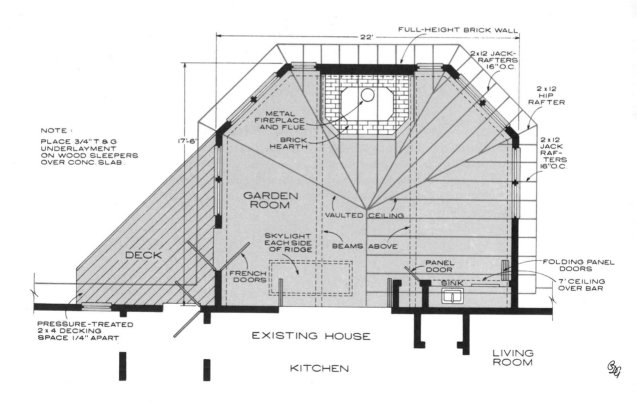

FULL-HEIGHT BRICK WALL

22'

2x12 JACK-RAFTERS 16" O.C.

2 x 12 HIP RAFTER

NOTE:
PLACE 3/4" T & G UNDERLAYMENT ON WOOD SLEEPERS OVER CONC. SLAB.

17'-6"

METAL FIREPLACE AND FLUE

BRICK HEARTH

2 x 12 JACK-RAFTERS 16" O.C.

GARDEN ROOM

VAULTED CEILING

DECK

SKYLIGHT EACH SIDE OF RIDGE

BEAMS ABOVE

PANEL DOOR

FOLDING PANEL DOORS

FRENCH DOORS

SINK

7' CEILING OVER BAR

PRESSURE-TREATED 2 x 4 DECKING SPACE 1/4" APART

EXISTING HOUSE

LIVING ROOM

KITCHEN

Note that the bar corner is boxed in with its own dropped ceiling. The flat "shelf" above is ideal for house plants, because it's directly under a large skylight.

With all its interior baffles (the faceted ceiling is faced with drywall and has fiberglass insulation above), the space is acoustically alive—ideal for listening to music. These homeowners have speakers tucked into end tables and hung on the wall, with the hi-fi gear concealed in the closet beside the bar.

This built-in bar makes the addition an ideal space for entertaining. Hosts never have to leave their guests to rustle up refreshments. The undercounter refrigerator keeps ice, mixers, and fresh fruit at hand, while the Kohler Gimlet bar sink eases preparation and cleanup. In fact, you can just stash used glassware on the sink counter and close the folding doors, leaving dishwashing for after guests have gone.

Because this new wing was spliced onto the existing kitchen, it is handy to serve dinner here, as well. All the windows are operable and equipped with interior screens; and in hot weather, they swing wide for the next best thing to the alfresco dining originally intended. In summer the deck adds another 200 square feet of space for large parties. Spotlights under the eaves keep the area festive after the sun sets.

The decking is pressure-treated 2 × 4s, spaced ¼-inch apart for drainage. As shown, the outer edge of the deck is projected from the 45-degree-angled wall of the garden room. This creates a deck area large enough to accommodate a small wrought-iron table and chair set, and because the structure bridges a corner of the house, it's easy to hang the joists from ledgers lag-screwed to the two walls of the house. Only two posts were needed to support the outer edge. For more space, of course, you could build the deck square.—*Text by Alfred Lees, photos by George Lyon.*

Appendix: Metric Makes Planking Easier

Metric measure may not have caught on with the do-it-yourselfer as expected, but I have found it's perfect for measurements that ordinarily require cumbersome manipulations of distances in feet, inches, and fractions of an inch.

Fractions can be especially unmanageable to the amateur. Millimeters, on the other hand, are easily managed on a pocket calculator. Use the calculator with a rule that's scaled in millimeters, and they do most of the work. I've found the 8-meter-long Lufkin Y38CME Ultralock to be a good choice among metric rules. You still have to provide the brainpower in laying out your work, of course, but a whole lot less of it.

An ideal use for metric measure is in planking a wood deck, as shown in the photos. You can use your calculator to determine the plank spacing so that it comes out even, in full-width boards. That way no planks have to be ripped, and there are no partial pieces at one end. The metric rule will help in actually doing the spacing.—*Text and photos by Richard Day.*

By converting to metric the dimensions of such construction work as laying out floors and decks, precision planning can be done on a calculator. To plank a deck, first take a measurement across the framing (top left photo), adding 25 mm at each end for an overhang.

 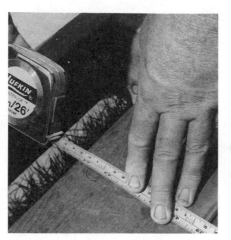 

Lay out a sample of five planks (left) with their edges tightly together, and measure across them. Divide that figure by the number of boards (5) to get the average board width. Calculate (middle) how many boards it will take to cover the deck, allowing three-mm gaps. If the result doesn't come out even, adjust the gap size so full-width boards will just fill. Use the calculator's constant function to determine the board positions from a single point of origin (right). The overhang will conceal any slight discrepancy.

Index